Paul Virilio and
Diller Scofidio + Renfro,
Mark Hansen, Laura Kurgan,
and **Ben Rubin,** in collaboration with
Robert Gerard Pietrusko and Stewart Smith

EXIT

A Work from the Collection of the
Fondation Cartier pour l'art contemporain

Fondation*Cartier*
pour l'art contemporain

Propelled by an idea of French philosopher and urbanist Paul Virilio, *EXIT* was created by American artists and architects, Diller Scofidio + Renfro, in collaboration with architect Laura Kurgan, statistician Mark Hansen, and designer Ben Rubin, along with Robert Gerard Pietrusko, Stewart Smith, and a core team of scientists.

The Fondation Cartier pour l'art contemporain presented *EXIT* for the first time in 2008, within the exhibition *Native Land, Stop Eject*, conceived with Paul Virilio and French photographer and filmmaker Raymond Depardon. Thinking about the exhibition project, Paul Virilio had the idea of an object that would offer a visualization of human trajectories across the globe, to show the evolution of economic, political, and environmental migrations in time and space. How could we realize this project? At the time, in 2006, there was nothing like it, not in museums, on television, or film. Then I thought of Elizabeth Diller and Ricardo Scofidio. I knew them as architects and artists, for they had participated in our exhibition *Un monde réel* in 1999; they were excellent with technology in an intuitive and inventive way. They knew Paul Virilio and admired his mind as an architect, philosopher, and urbanist. For us, that point was decisive if we were to build a team devoted to this ambitious project. And in fact, the affinity between them was immediate.

We thus built different teams, in New York and in Paris, including François Gemenne, a specialist in environmental migrations, a little-known discipline at the time. Elizabeth Diller and her team responded brilliantly, knowing what was at stake: an artwork combining strong aesthetics and information, a real tool with the capacity of

Introduction

by Hervé Chandès

**General Director,
Fondation Cartier pour l'art contemporain, Paris**

evolving over time. Altogether, thanks to the collaboration of many international organizations and research centers, a masterpiece emerged: a dynamic presentation of the data documenting contemporary human movements displayed in an immersive space that presents a 360-degree projection of five animated maps. Despite many technical difficulties and challenges, we succeeded, thanks to our determination, and the result met Paul Virilio's expectations. For the first time, a cultural institution took on contemporary issues and provided the public with an artistic object of knowledge.

EXIT was very well received by the general public, as well as by academic, scientific, governmental, and associative organizations. At the time, the art world was not yet fully embracing the installation's purpose. It was to be a few years before exhibitions dedicated to the world's human and environmental issues began appearing. Then, *EXIT* was presented during COP15 in Copenhagen in 2009; its reception was far from what we'd hoped. Still, in 2010, a new map was created for the inauguration of the Alhóndiga Bilbao with the collaboration of anthropologist Bruce Albert and contributors from all over the world: *Speechless and Deforestation*. And in 2015, *EXIT* was fully updated for its presentation at the Palais de Tokyo in Paris during COP21, where it met with resounding success.

This book tells the story of this timely, informative, and compelling artwork, which joined the Collection of the Fondation Cartier in 2012. Meant to evolve constantly, following the major changes of the contemporary world, *EXIT* is an infinite artwork that provides the rare opportunity to question our responsibility toward humankind.

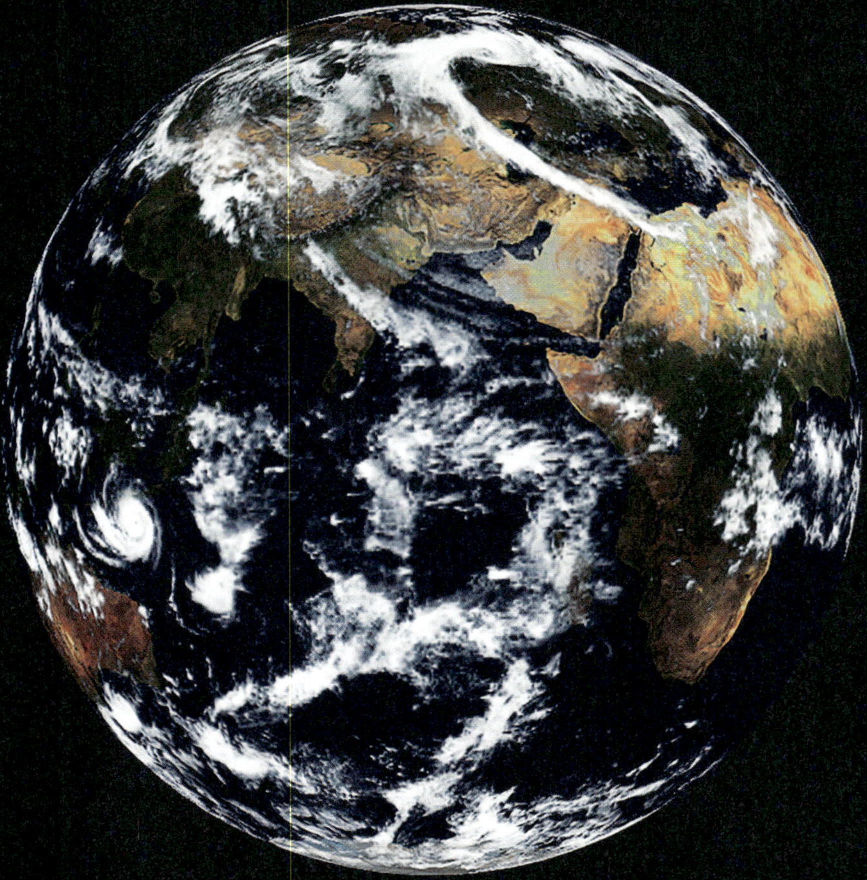

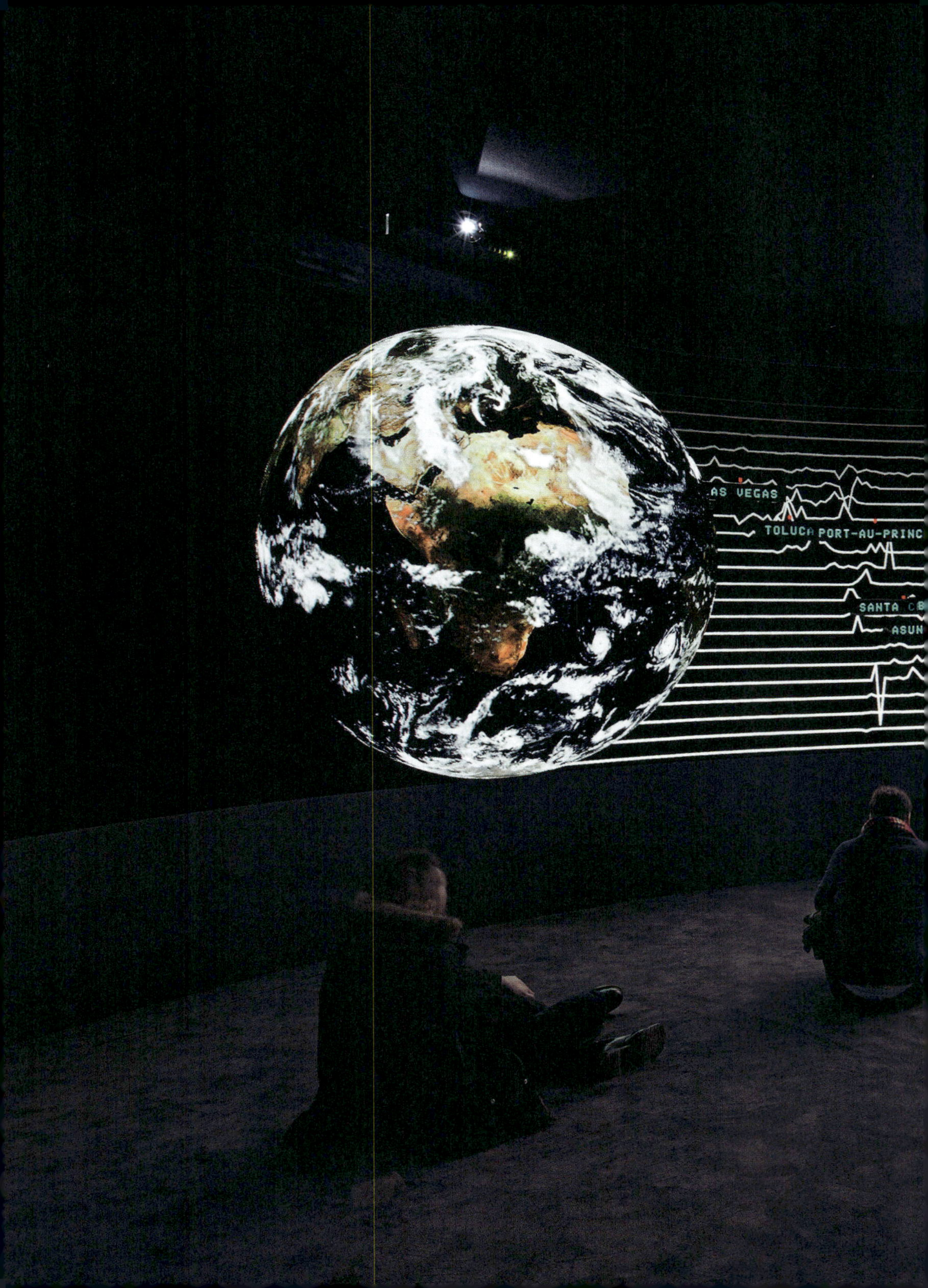
AS VEGAS
TOLUCA
PORT-AU-PRINC
SANTA
ASUN

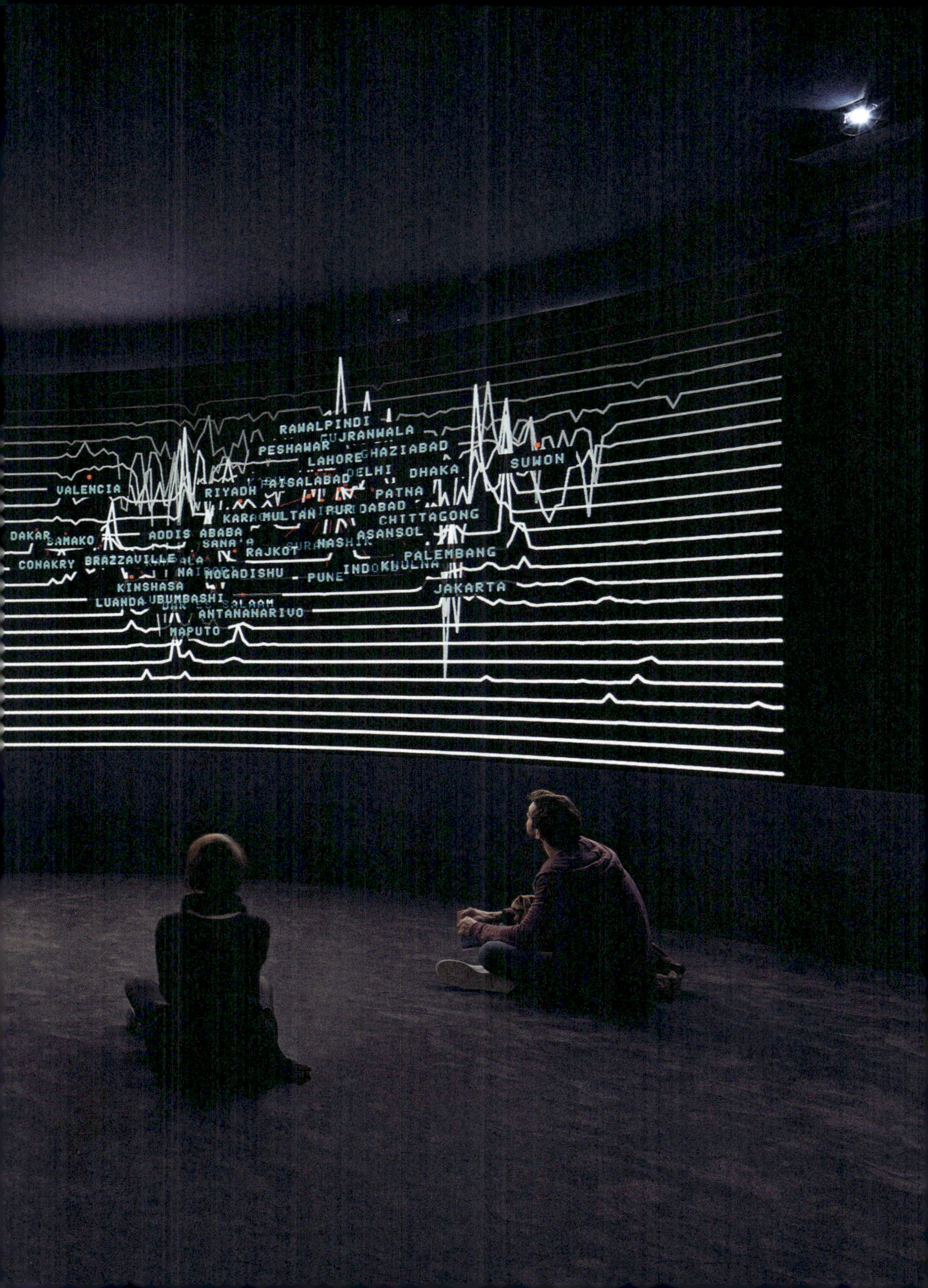
RAWALPINDI
PESHAWAR
LAHORE
GHAZIABAD
DELHI
DHAKA
SUWON
VALENCIA
RIYADH
PATNA
CHITTAGONG
DAKAR
ADDIS ABABA
SANA'A
ASANSOL
RAJKOT
CONAKRY
BRAZZAVILLE
PALEMBANG
MOGADISHU
PUNE
JAKARTA
KINSHASA
LUANDA
ANTANANARIVO
MAPUTO

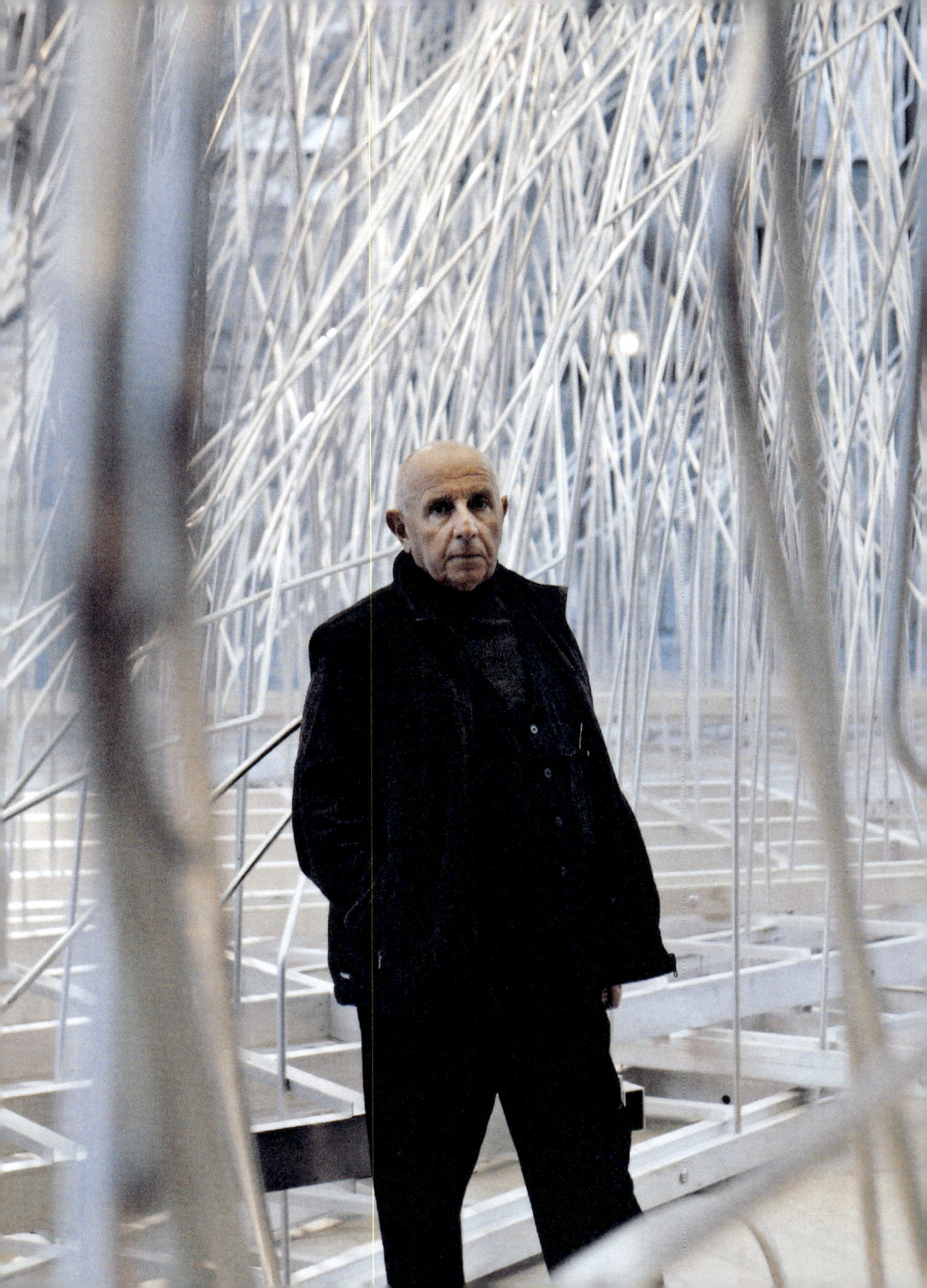

STOP EJECT

by Paul Virilio

> Out of here—that's my goal.
> FRANZ KAFKA

According to a report published in 2007 by the British NGO Christian Aid, the number of future environmental migrants is estimated at close to one billion. In the view of this document, 645 million people will be displaced from their homes over the next forty years because of large-scale development projects, such as intensive mining activity and the building of hydroelectric dams. Of these people, 250 million will be displaced by phenomena related to climate change, floods, and submersion of coastal land and, ultimately, at least 50 million people will be displaced by conflicts produced by such catastrophic upheavals entailing the demographic resettlement of the planet.

Faced with this unprecedented migration crisis, which is incomparably more serious than the immigration of the industrial age, and which is already being called the *migration offensive* of the third millennium, the issue of urbanization in the contemporary world might be seen in terms that torpedo the customary distinction between SEDENTARINESS and NOMADISM.

In fact, after the pluralist era of sustainable settlement of registered urban land—a setting that once, in antiquity, introduced the notion of "citizenship," as deriving from political localization, and with it, ultimately, of the "legally constituted state" of nations—the era of habitable human *traffic* is now kicking off with this transpolitical delocalization now torpedoing the GEOPOLITICS of settlement in the age of globalization. And this is happening at the precise moment that the teletechnologies of information are ensuring that the *sedentary human*

← Paul Virilio in front of *The Fall* (2002) by Lebbeus Woods. Exhibition *Unknown Quantity*, Fondation Cartier pour l'art contemporain, Paris, 2002

is at home everywhere, and *the nomad*, nowhere, beyond the provisional accommodation offered by a now pointless transhumance. That transhumance now takes place not only from one country to another; now people are displaced within their very homeland from their heartland to some vague territory where refugee camps have not only taken over from the SHANTY TOWNS of days gone by, but from the TOWNS. The megalopolis of the excluded of all stripes, who pour in from all sides, has now come to rival the all-too real megalopolis of the included, the ULTRACITY.

The exoticism of misery thereby meets the exoticism of happy tourism, and it is not hard to imagine the scale of such a telescoping of these groups of people who have come adrift from their moorings in urbanity, as they did once, not so long ago, from their customary moorings in rurality. It is not hard to imagine, either, the scale of any traffic accident now that the traffic is no longer local, as it was in the days of the great invasions, but global.

Allowed to travel since 1997, 37 million Chinese left their homeland last year. When the 2008 Olympic Games are over, you can bet that as many as 70 million will turn into tourists.

Note on that score that there has long been a *floating population* of close to 100 million destitute peasants in China, wandering around looking for work and most often winding up in the country's vast railway stations. As Chen Guidi and Wu Chuntao say peasants were kept out of the towns at the end of the 1950s by means of the grain supply scheme and Mao Zedong's institution of a RESIDENT'S PASSBOOK—the HUKOW—which divided society into two classes: urban and rural ... From that point on, *town and country would be like two vehicles travelling on different tracks*.[1]

After the "sustainable" settlement that characterized the population flows of past history, "habitable" human traffic opens up dizzying perspectives for planetary resettlement.

Having first lost its suburbs and then its hinterland, the METACITY of tomorrow won't long be able to resist the demographic pressure coming from its OUTLAND, which will drive the exodus of settlers without hope of returning to the sedentariness of the *semi-autonomous city* of our origins.

It is hard, in fact, to imagine the radiant future of "sustainable development" in the face of the RACKET made by communications and tele-

---

1. Chen Guidi and Wu Chuntao, *Will the Boat Sink the Water?: The Life of China's Peasants*, trans. Zhu Hong (New York: Public Affairs, 2006).

communications tools that are undeniably progressive, but also completely incapable of dealing with the transpolitical tragedy of ecology.

These tools can no more deal with the greenhouse gas effect on the *atmosphere*, than with the effect on the *dromosphere* of the mass exodus of idle masses. Forget the INSTANT.CITY that the English Futurists imagined. What developers now have in mind is a NON-STOP CIRCUS, a long-haul cruise for the exiles of outsourcing. This is the "war of each against all," the ultimate figure of a sort of *civil war of movement* that would take over from the *siege war* of the Commune or of the underprivileged suburban outskirts. Actually, what we are now seeing, as the third millennium gets under way, is the emergence of an absolutely unknown form of exterritorialization of human potential that is soon likely to rule out all possibility of any kind of *urban potential*. This will lead to a new form of EX.CENTRICITY, whereby the quest for an EXOPLANET, an ULTRAWORLD, as a replacement for the old one, now too polluted, will double up, here below, with the quest for an ULTRACITY, a sort of logistics platform, of which the airport, the port, and the railway station, have only ever been scaled-down models.

Abandoning the right to citizenship by virtue of birth in a country defined by geopolitics and the historic persistence of sites, the *portable revolution* will complete the transport revolution and *the revolution in transmission* will land us in this interactive PLANISPHERE that will, they say, be able to supplement the too tight BIOSPHERE and its five continents. It will do this thanks to the feats in information technology of a virtual continent, the great colony of cyberspace taking over from the empires of yore.

*

EMERGENCY EXIT. If the major event of the moment for anthropologists is demographic growth over the past century—from one and a half billion individuals in 1900 to six billion in the year 2000—when this is coupled with the boom in instantaneous transmission and supersonic transport, the result will be one billion displaced people tomorrow, deportees everywhere you look. We'll need to somehow rehouse these people and we'll need to do so in less than half a century. That seems quite simply impossible to achieve unless ... unless we abandon the city, the *semi-autonomous town*, and go back to encampments, and the precariousness of "temporary housing."

In 1900, *rural exodus* was in full swing in the West and one in ten of the planet's inhabitants was a city dweller. Today, it is one in two; in other words, four times the 1950 number. That means there are three billion sedentary metropolitans—at the very moment that urban exodus is kicking off with the prospect of those one billion dispossessed refugees by the year 2050 ...

After the general mobilization of the Great War, which was a direct result of the ideology of the "people in arms," and the total mobilization of the Second World War, what is being foreshadowed in this great economic and ecological transhumance is not so much the final struggle as the *integral mobilization* of populations driven from their native land and from GEOLOCALIZATION. This was before the latter mutated into a mere matter of satellite positioning (GPS or GALILEO), but was still the most important political event in the history of humanity, whereby the HIC ET NUNC of geopolitics were tied in together with the City of our origins, the POLIS with its "right to citizenship based on birth in a country" as opposed to the "right of citizenship based on kinship" upheld by nomadic tribes. All this just to give shape to the PLACE (*LIEU*) of the SOCIAL BOND (*LIEN*) and of a "common right" that used to be expressed perfectly well, as it happens, by the AXIS MUNDI of the cities of antiquity which represented the *center of the world*.

But let's get back to the sudden drift set off by a depopulation process through which EXURBANISM is gearing up to supplant the SUBURBANISM of the outskirts of the industrial era. At the end of 2007, the cities of La Haye and Rotterdam alone were facing an influx of 40,000 new migrants. The idea of setting up CONTAINERS to accommodate Polish laborers was being touted ... Nobody was put off by such a blatantly segregationist practice at local government level in relation to *foreigners* from the Eastern European Community. In Amsterdam, for instance, the now famous containers on the port where dockers once used to get together, today already house Dutch students; and Algeco, the maker and operator of on-site sheds which recently bought out its American subsidiary Williams Scotsman, has become the world leader in modular space solutions.

We might note in passing that, now that the great race to speed up progress has been won by instantaneous transmission equipment, all that transport equipment has to offer is the slight advantage of a growing and still indispensable CARRYING CAPACITY. Yet the constraints due to dwindling petrol supplies and growing pollution will shortly necessitate restrictions on movement and an exponential growth in quantities carried since the logics or, more exactly, the logistics, of a just-in-time distribution system now entail gigantism in loads to the detriment of the old warehouses. Whence the endlessly increasing importance of the *intermodal platform* in freight transportation. Today intermodal platforms ensure transit, and break-of-load between one means of transport and another, whether land, sea, or air. They do this for the "bulk carriers," the vast container ships, that serve the different quarters of the ULTRACITY under construction, this "capital to end all capitals" thrown up by international economic integration.

So, it is well and truly under way, this sort of post-urban revolution that will drive the twenty-first century. It is a PORTABLE REVOLUTION with consequences for the history of planning and development that could prove singularly more devastating than last century's revolution in industrial transport. This is why, right now, the rug is being pulled out from under sedentary settlement of an *urban species* which is, in the end, as threatened as the rural species was up until the revelation of food insecurity that has now hit us, with the totally symptomatic business of BIOFUELS based on cereal and maize.

As Heidermarie Wieczorek, the German Minister for Economic Cooperation and Development, recently put it: "The right to food takes precedence over the right to mobility." In fact, the sudden emergence of the ULTRACITY is incomparably more frightening in its sociopolitical implications than is the contemporary urban sprawl triggered by the boom in the domestic automobile.

With EXURBIA gearing up to outpace old SUBURBIA and its tentacular conurbations, we hardly flinch anymore over the importance enterprises now give to OUTSOURCING production—including research and development—to the detriment of their former patrimonial localization. And so, for some little time now, *the external* has been winning hands down over *the internal* everywhere you turn, and geophysical history has been turned inside out like a glove!

Whence the successive generations of "portable" objects, whereas objects were once happy to be "fixed" and precisely situated. Whence also, as I've pointed out elsewhere, the radical reversal of the relationship between NOMADISM and SEDENTARINESS that is at the origins of settlement. Now accompanying baggage far outweighs vehicles of all kinds, with computers, cell phones, electronic transponder bracelets, and GPS, the watch that now tells the PLACE the way the old one told the TIME. These devices anticipate the implants of the transplantation age, such as the Radio Frequency Identification tag, a microchip GPS tracking implant. As we all know: every time the speed of movement increases, monitoring and traceability increase in step.

A bit further down the track, IDENTITY will give way to the TRACEABILITY of the private citizen, of any distinct person, just as the CNIL, the *Commission nationale de l'informatique et des libertés*, already fears is happening.

Just like the elementary particle at the heart of Geneva's Great Accelerator—the Large Hadron Collider—we will then not only be "filed," but tracked, making knowing where we permanently reside completely pointless.

"The automobile made us people without home," mused Adorno many moons ago. What can we say, today, in the age of the spreading portability that is now taking over from the political participation of the past century, except that the "escape velocity" generated by technical progress turns us into DEPORTEES of a new kind. And that this leads directly not to the extermination of GENOCIDE, but to the GEOCIDE of externalization—the OUTSOURCING—of "urbankind" and, soon, of humankind in general. The pathological sequelae of this are unknown. The myth of some happy, beneficial neo-nomadism won't long survive the experience of being locked down in a closed circuit, within the now relative non-expanse of this life-bearing star of ours.

A veritable astronomic revolution in the historic CONTINUUM, the globalization of post-industrial interactivity literally turns the complex orientation of human activity on its head. Whence the abuse of the terms "deregulation" and "relocation." Whence also the repeat divorces afflicting the "urbankind" of our once "civilized" societies, as well as the whole array of foreign policies, now discredited in the name of an eccentric planetary globalization. This process is aided and abetted, we might note in passing, by certain astrophysicists who hide behind the pretext of pollution of the earthly environment to pride themselves on being able to discover, somewhere in the universe, a SUPER EARTH, likely, in its gigantic dimensions, to provide a positive response to the negative ecological footprint that Mother Earth faces, with the damage done by progress, our tiny little telluric planet finally proving insalubrious and unfit for life.

We must point out here that this quest for an exoplanet entails a quest for an ULTRAWORLD to come, which will suddenly shoot out like a cosmic model of the ULTRACITY, thereby reversing the very notion of symbolic centrality with the sedentariness of the geophysical HIC ET NUNC.

For if the Axis of the World ran through the heart of the city of antiquity, yesterday, tomorrow the ULTRACITY—the Metacity—will be outsourced to the middle of nowhere!

*

"Deportation" yesterday, "exclusion" today—both terms define a semantic slide that signals, if not exodus, then at least forced exile. It is an expression of a truly "repulsive" globalization that no one can now contest, as though last century's mass tourism had only been an early warning sign of the dispossession to come, a sort of warm-up, getting the hordes ready for the ordeal of an off-track trip, with leisurely wayfaring far from home foreshadowing the takeoff out of this world offered by space tourism, with a view to one day securing the public salvation of humanity! And so, following last century's destruction and mass extermination, Time, the "real time" of social deconstruction, seems to be upon us, with its forced externalization, or outsourcing.

"Going and seeing elsewhere," and "seeing it coming" right here—this alternating movement seems to endlessly accelerate, oscillating between the initially exotic impulse and the expulsion of those excluded from an international integration that is now terminal and not inaugural, as it once was at, say, the time of the discovery of the Americas.

In fact, geophysical space is no longer *an adjustment variable* for the economy of our displacements, as it was in the era of past international population flows.

Here again, the reversal is evident, since the famous "End of History" is barely more than an optical (dromoscopic) illusion that mainly marks the end of geography and its continuum. The mass portable revolution is only the ultimate consequence of the portability involved in acceleration of reality and of the exhaustion of the resources produced by the GEODIVERSITY of a globe that cannot go on much longer sustaining the exhaustion of time distances. If you listen to the travel agents, our contemporaries cannot possibly be considered "catastrophists" since "tour operators are booked out." Naturally, today's tourists are not pessimists in the manner of the well-heeled voyagers of bygone days who traveled for pleasure. It is worse. What they're beginning to feel is good old-fashioned cabin fever, the *claustrophobia* experienced by those buried alive by their own "carbon footprint"!

Don't they say that volunteer guinea pigs are already training to survive the long voyage to the planet Mars, vicariously, in an airtight compartment onboard a CONTAINER designed to familiarize them with the tedious and painful escape of long-haul exile that could well turn out to be one-way?

Actually, the current academic quarrel among astrophysicists over the comparative advantages of ROBOTIC PROBES of the "Mars Express" type, as opposed to MANNED FLIGHTS, illustrates perfectly how powerfully motivated the apostles of the revolution in portability to the ULTRAWORLD are. Whence the dubious appeal of the "lunar module," that container that can do anything but is especially good at undoing statics, the stability of being rooted in one's native soil, and promoting instead the eccentricity of a NON.STOP RACE.

After all, we did see an apple-green container only a little while ago, in Paris, did we not? It sat on the terrace of the Musée d'Art Moderne at the top of the Palais de Tokyo, opposite the Musée des arts premiers. Baptized the Hotel Everland, the little green box was designed to be rented out as a night-time shelter.

Similarly, following the CAPSULE HOTEL, designed by Japanese architect Kisho Kurokawa, Gatwick and Heathrow airports, both close to London, now offer their clientele the "Yotel," cylindrical cabins 8 square meters in size, placed flush with the ground, within the terminal buildings, for the benefit of (supernumerary) transit passengers.

Note that once again, it is not just the performance of the Stock Exchange that suddenly gets de-coupled from the real economy, now stripped of any relation to paper money every bit as much as to the nature of housing stock clearly in crisis. Today it is actually the whole of the political economy of nations that is suffering from the excesses of a catastrophic race for instant profit. They say we need to relativize any approach to or analysis of this situation that might be considered "geopolitical," so as to free ourselves from LOCALITY and, in the near future, even from the too tight territorial GLOBALITY of the earthly star.

With this in mind, we can get a better measure of the relationships of cause and effect at play in the mass exile of populations, starting with the most vulnerable, but ending, soon, we anticipate, in the headlong rush of the well-heeled, whose ambulatory madness as tourists is only ever a clinical symptom of loss of bearings or sudden disorientation. The subprime mortgage crisis in the United States, after all, illustrates to perfection the crisis in the construction and public works industries, with firms involved anticipating disaster in the stability of real estate, right here and now, by diversifying their activities and opting into so-called "booming sectors," such as motorway franchises, media, and energy outlets and, of course, hulking industrial-scale port facilities whose infrastructure will very soon be swamped by the requirements of the high-volume traffic and gigantic "load transfers" involved, CONTAINER CARRIERS and other methane-fueled tankers never ceasing to swell, to grow in obesity.

Just-in-time, that adage of intercontinental flow, does damage to the places where break-of-load between transport and the portable occurs.

After the transformation of dockyards into industrial wasteland—in Liverpool, London, Hamburg, Amsterdam—it is no longer the architecture of the warehouse that is now feeling the impact of the bulk carriers and their logistics. It is now the urbanism of cities on the HORIZONTAL littoral of loading and unloading zones. But it is also, equally, the urbanism of airport "hubs" on a littoral that is now VERTICAL. This is to say nothing of railway stations, which have gradually morphed into transit metropolises, terminals in the end ungovernable, as we see in Paris, Berlin, or Moscow.

*

"I've never had an objective. I'm a path, not a goal." So said Daniel Libeskind, the man responsible for the reconstruction of the "Ground Zero" site in New York.

Coming from an architect, that is a real revelation of the decline of static, of material resistance, and of the fixity of real estate that not so long ago characterized the persistence of the city.

Thus, the adage of the builders of the city of antiquity—PLOT.DIVIDE INTO LOTS.BUILD—needs to be replaced by PLOT.DIVIDE INTO LOTS. GET OUT, now that the vanishing line of the trajectory is supplanting the fixed point, and the objective axiality of the city.

And so, development of the Marseille quarter of Saint-Charles prompts the operations manager for the new unit (which now links the railway and bus terminals) to say: "This historic notion of a STATION is old hat. Saint-Charles terminal must, of course, remain a transport center, but it must eventually become a TOWN CENTER." Yet again, that about sums it up. The center of the ULTRACITY is now called on to supplant the age-old TOWN CENTER and to do so within a "just-in-time" dynamic that, after the rural exodus of the nineteenth and twentieth centuries, will lead to an *urban exodus* destined, in the twenty-first century, to achieve the EXURBANISM of resettlement of the world.

"Without a doubt, the United States has entered a new era in transportation," the US Secretary of Transportation, Norman Mineta, declared in 2002, at a conference on homeland security, referring to an era where "a cunning and remorseless enemy can challenge one of America's most cherished freedoms: freedom of movement."

Despite the deceptive appearances of international terrorism in the year 2001, but also of the terrorism directed at Atocha railway station in Madrid in 2004, the enemy is firstly the sphere of acceleration of reality, this DROMOSPHERE that will soon be able to do away with expanse in this latest of historic globalizations. Whence the cabin fever presented by a humanity now deprived of a future, and instead faced with the foreclosure of the spacetime of the common world, in a lockdown that is both carceral and panoptic, in which the GLOBALITARIANISM of progress will come to mean control of movement, of displacement flow.

In what would be the antithesis of the "radiant future" touted by the totalitarianisms of yore, the mobile home and the endless non-stop tour will take over from the semiautonomous city and the CLAUSTROPOLIS will dominate the ancient COSMOPOLIS everywhere you look. And so, after the *futurism of long-term History* that sprang up in the twentieth century, denounced by Daniel Lévy and celebrated by F. T. Marinetti, the time would then be upon us of this *futurism of the instant*, which Octavio Paz spoke to us about, observing bitterly: "The moment is uninhabitable, just like the future."

So it is this form of insalubrious UNINHABITING that today speaks to us through the exoduses, through the distant exiles, through all this dislocation that is only ever deportation in disguise—not, as once upon a time, propelling people towards the extermination of the camps, toward GENOCIDE, anymore, but driving them towards the externalization, the OUTSOURCING, of the ultracity to come, towards the GEOCIDE of the twilight of places, and the exhaustion of the resources provided by the geodiversity of the terrestrial globe.

"We are all deep in a hell each moment of which is a miracle," Cioran noted,[2] thereby describing the very latest of futurisms: acceleration of reality in the twenty-first century.

Here we touch on the now critical issue of *the political economy of speed*—or, rather, its denial by the experts of a macrofinancial system whereby the political economy of wealth and speculation has been trans-

---

2. E. M. Cioran, *The New Gods*, trans. Richard Howard (Chicago, IL: University of Chicago Press, [1969] 2013), p. 120.

ferred to SOFTWARE PACKAGES, mathematical automatons. For these latter, space is absolutely not an adjustment variable anymore, since they only work through this "miracle" of the futurism of the instant—in other words, through the miracle of a "transfer accident," or the imposture of immediacy, which excludes all expanse just as it does all true duration and with it, the rational intelligence behind the geopolitics of nations.

Speaking of this "hell," at the bottom of which we all repose thanks to the prowess of the demiurges of the world economy, let's hear it from a judge handling illegal immigration cases in Europe: "We're in danger of shortly being dragged into a diabolical cycle. It sends shivers down your spine when you learn, for example, that some migrants cut off their fingers to avoid having their fingerprints taken and identified."

When you know that around 20 million people apply for entry to the Schengen area every year, you get an idea of the growing size of the mass movement of a population easily set adrift from their social moorings as well as their territorial ties. You also get an idea of the growing importance of a sort of "large-scale battue," a hunt for civilians, which extends the rural exodus of the final years of the second millennium into the third, and, especially, the long convoys going east in the mass deportation of populations that preceded their pure and simple extermination. For the new "war on civilians" no longer only uses railways and the *shunting yards* they come with, but *charter flights*, in a bid to enforce a mass displacement brought on by the evil spells of unbearable progress that are every bit as economic as they are ecological.

Whence the draconian border controls put in place by customs officers and border patrols, with the biometric passport supplanting the old identity card, and soon to be itself supplanted by the credit card, as though the power to purchase had once and for all taken over from the power to dwell somewhere together.

*

In fact, the lack of delay, of any interval of time, that now characterizes macroeconomic systems in the era of interactive globalization does not so much ratchet up competition between nations, as the World Trade Organization would have us believe. It tends more to induce the opening of hostilities between civilian populations now threatened on all sides—confrontations in which RESETTLEMENT of the terrestrial globe is now such an urgent issue that soon no metropolitan geopolitics will be able to deal with it.

To try to go beyond the sovereignty of nations in favor of sovereign wealth funds would clearly mean destroying the DOMICILIARY INERTIA of History in the near future, thereby triggering a fatal process of deconstruction—deconstruction of the city and of a "metropolitics" that stood surety for a strictly territorial legitimate state. This would promote, instead, a few BRANCH SITES, hinted at by the "artificial earthly paradises" and condominiums that are today dotted around here and there, with the insularity of urban land making way for archipelagos of private islands, such as in Dubai and elsewhere. But they won't hold out, any more than the "resettlement camps," against this TSUNAMI of panic-stricken hordes, this human tidal wave of close to a billion exiles that no one will be able to decently house in under half a century.

So, let's not be under any illusions. What is happening in Africa and Asia, with the 50 million people qualified by the Office of the United Nations High Commissioner for Refugees as "victims of forced displacement," is only ever a clinical symptom of *the freeing up of housing* currently under way that will in turn strike Europe and the Americas and the rest of the developed world, for as a French author writes: "There is no outside, no physical space between the global and the sum of all the nation states."[3] And the so-called "transitory towns" of the refugee camps will never turn into authentic cities—no matter what their demography—anymore than the shanty towns turned into true working-class suburban outskirts.

Here a revealing figure is called for: during the First World War, mobilization set some 65 million men in motion. Well, currently, the number is practically the same, since that figure of 50 million clearly does not include the invisible mass of undocumented people, who are the missing energy of the expanding world of populations in exile.

General mobilization in the twentieth century, global mobilization on the cusp of the twenty-first. After the *siege war* of the Paris Commune in the nineteenth century, the *civilian displacement war* has just broken out. This war dissolves the notions of CENTER and PERIPHERY in these days of mass displacement, whereby economic rationales to do with "purchasing power" or "dwelling power" have become interchangeable in the exclusion of a world where the workforce has, it would seem, lost its civilizing value and bows out before the madness of electronic automation of production.

---

3. Michel Agier, *On the Margins of the World: The Refugee Experience Today*, trans. David Fernbach (Cambridge: Polity, 2008).

What is shaping up here, in this universe that is much busier *excluding* than *expanding*, is no longer, no matter what they say, the return of the COSMOPOLIS, or even of the CLAUSTROPOLIS of gated communities or high-rise towers. What is shaping up, above all, is the MARSHALLING YARD, this "terminus of last wishes" that Cendrars talked about in the *Prose of the Trans-Siberian*.

This is the revelation of a fundamentally transpolitical ULTRACITY, where the habitable staying-put of bygone days has abandoned public space to parking lots, and to the uninhabitable human traffic of each against all. This is the universal civil war in which the trajectory of real-time exchanges has supplanted the PLACE (*LIEU*) and the SOCIAL BOND (*LIEN*) of domiciliation.

On that score, let's hear it from Emmanuel Levinas:

"The world in which reason becomes more and more self-conscious is not habitable. It is ... like those supply depots where merchandise which cannot satisfy is piled up ... it is impersonal, like factory hangars ... where manufactured things remain abstract, true with the truth of calculation and brought into the anonymous circuit of the economy."[4]

That's it, the "digital break" in which the reign of quantity is mobilized to sweep away everything in its path, in the name of immediate profit, that veritable GEOCRUISER of an astronomical financial history, in which the just-in-time delivery systems of the closed circuit of the world economy turn the warehouse, the abandoned dock, into the latest vehicle in a "great movement" of Progress that destroys, one by one, the statics of common places, along with the stability of social bonds.

This is the futurism of an uninhabitable instant, just as Octavio Paz predicted, confirming Emmanuel Levinas's philosophy. It is a progressivism in which it is not so much a matter of leaving in order to get there safe and sound, anymore, as it is of getting out in order to clear the terrain, and heading for a future "twilight of places," which, for want of limiting borders between states, now offers nothing more than the catastrophe of continental portals for the greater profit of smugglers pouring in from everywhere.

Text first published in the exhibition catalog
Native Land, Stop Eject (Paris: Fondation Cartier
pour l'art contemporain, 2008)
Translated from the French by Julie Rose

---

4. Emmanuel Levinas, "Judaism and Feminism," in *Difficult Freedom: Essays on Judaism*, trans. Sean Hand (Baltimore, MD: Johns Hopkins University Press, 1990), p. 32.

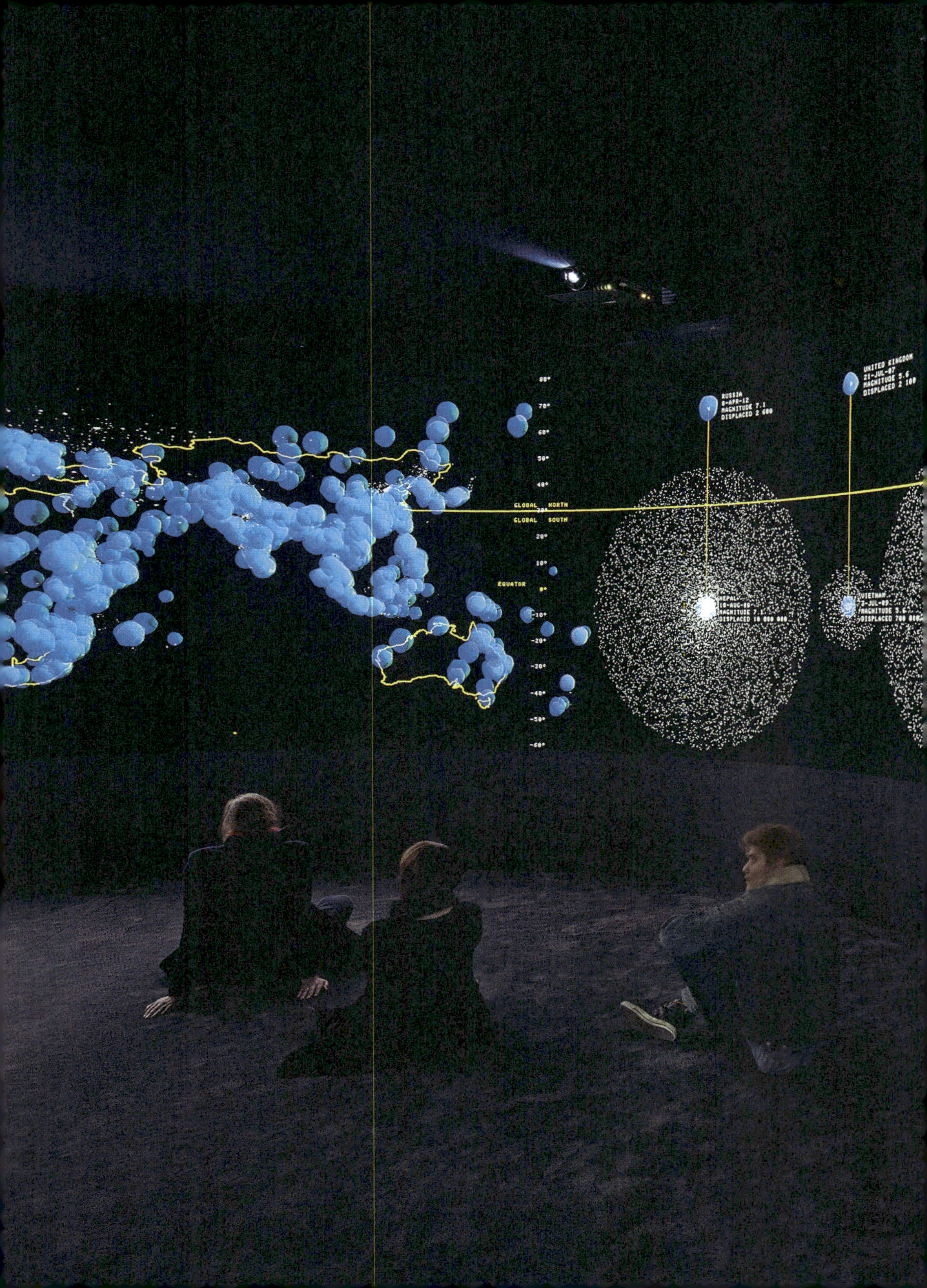
UNITED KINGDOM
21-JUL-07
MAGNITUDE 5.6
DISPLACED 2 100
RUSSIA
8-APR-12
MAGNITUDE 7.1
DISPLACED 2 600
80°
70°
60°
50°
40°
GLOBAL NORTH
GLOBAL SOUTH
20°
10°
EQUATOR
0°
-10°
-20°
-30°
-40°
NEPAL
18-AUG-08
MAGNITUDE 7.1
DISPLACED 10 000 000
VIETNAM
3-JUL-09
MAGNITUDE 5.6
-50°
-60°

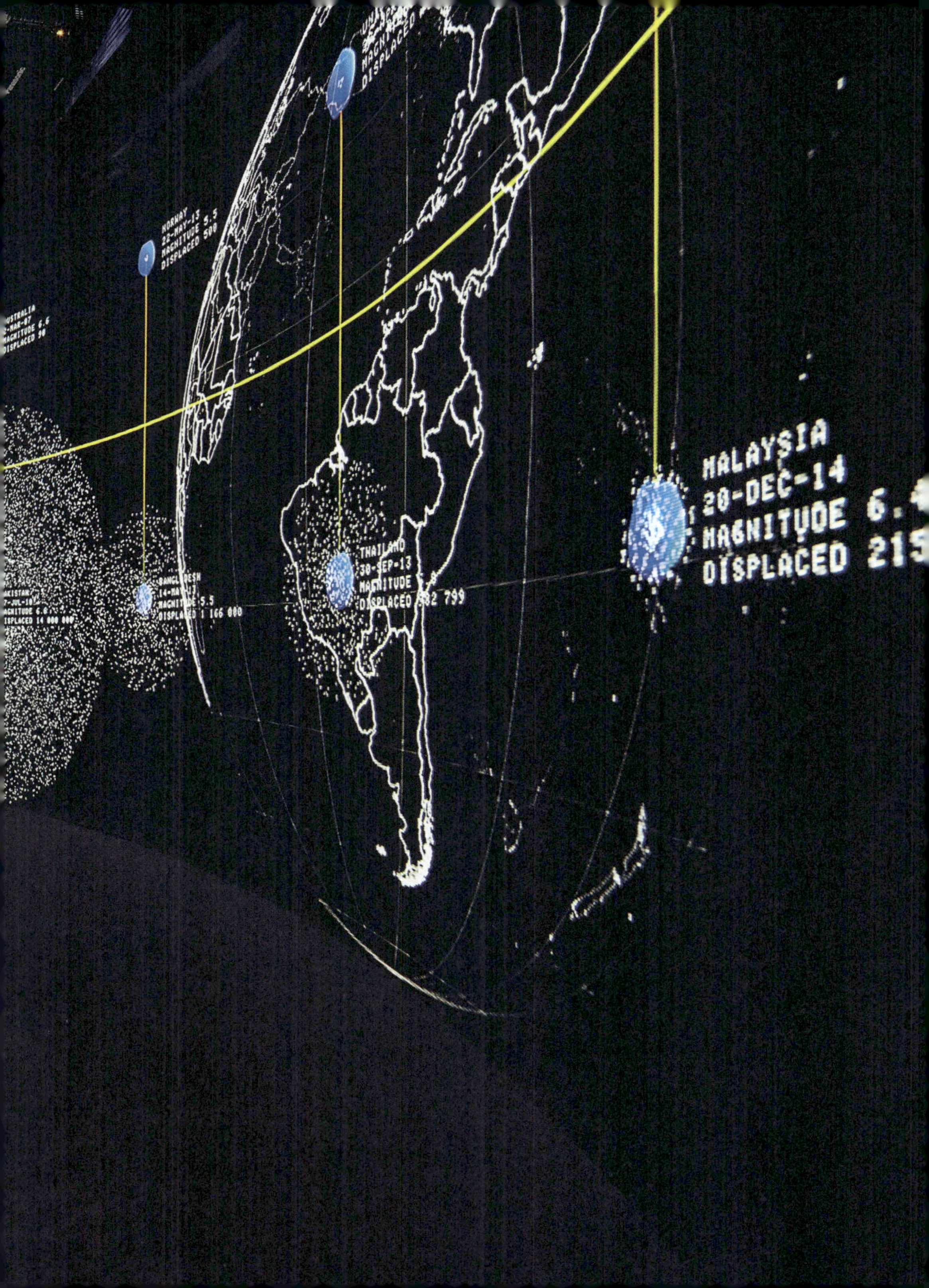
NORWAY
22-MAY-13
MAGNITUDE 5.5
DISPLACED 500
THAILAND
30-SEP-13
MAGNITUDE
MALAYSIA
20-DEC-14
MAGNITUDE 6.
DISPLACED 21

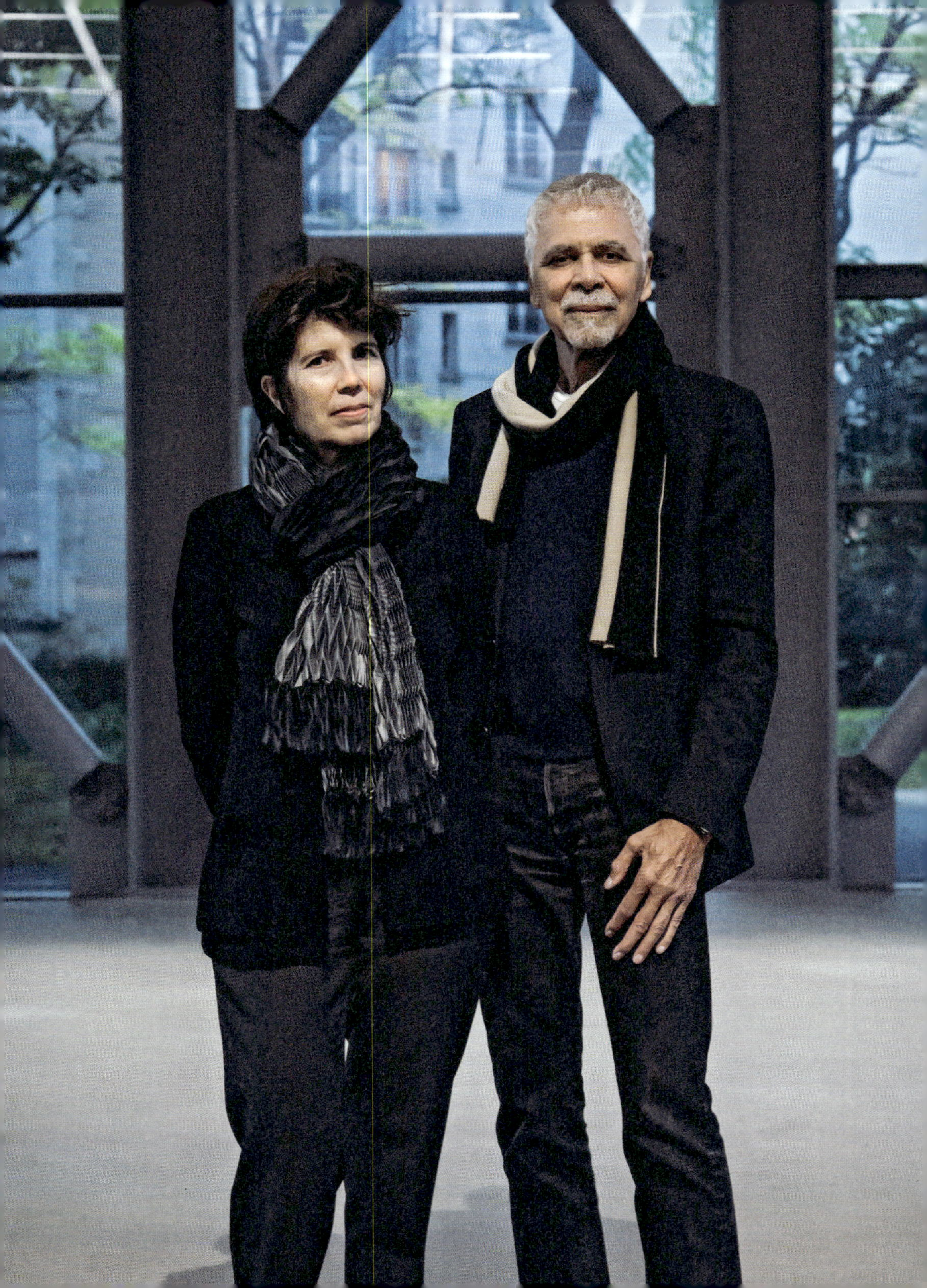

Interview with Elizabeth Diller

by Grazia Quaroni

Director of Collections,
Fondation Cartier pour l'art contemporain, Paris

Grazia Quaroni: Let's start by going back to the very beginnings of *EXIT*: Hervé Chandès was working with Paul Virilio on an exhibition called *Native Land, Stop Eject*, scheduled for 2008, and he visited you in New York. He knew you were Paul Virilio readers, that you were interested in his ideas, and that you both knew the Fondation Cartier very well. Could you describe that first meeting?

Elizabeth Diller: I remember my excitement about the prospect of working with Paul Virilio, and explaining that he was a contentious figure in academic circles, whose world view could be interpreted in two ways: utopian or dystopian. He was against the dogma of technological progress but was interested in technology itself. I had always chosen to read his work through the battle between the two, rather than the more reductive lens of the two polar extremes.

And then we talked about how Paul Virilio inspired *Jet Lag*, a theatrical work we initiated in 1998 that was coproduced by the Maison des Arts in Créteil. It was based on a reference in one of Virilio's books to an American grandmother who kidnapped her grandson to escape the boy's father, who wanted him to get psychiatric treatment for his antisocial behavior. To protect the kid, she flew back and forth with him from New York to Amsterdam over 160 times continuously, with the occasional night at the airport. She finally died of jet lag. Paul Virilio called her "a contemporary heroine who lived in deferred time."

The story seemed dubious. I had a hard time believing that you could die of jet lag, or that anyone flew back and forth across the Atlantic

← Elizabeth Diller and Ricardo Scofidio,
Fondation Cartier pour l'art contemporain, Paris, 2014

that many times. I looked everywhere for references to this woman and couldn't find a thing. I figured Virilio must have invented the story, so I called him up. He said it was true and gave me the correct spelling of her name. And there it was: a long-forgotten *New York Times* story from 1971 calling her the Flying Granny. This woman was the protagonist of our performance that was about making a home in constant motion.

Paul Virilio saw and loved *Jet Lag* and we bonded. So we were delighted that Hervé and Paul thought of us to imagine a work about human mobility.

GQ: And how was your initial meeting with Paul Virilio in Paris? His idea was to show human trajectories across the globe, realizing that these are mostly linked to climate, economy, and politics. What shape did your first discussions take?

ED: He actually didn't impose any strategies on us. It was wide open. He prompted our work by framing the mobility of people for three causes: political, economic, and environmental. In our first meeting we were probing human migration in its many forms. People moving across national borders not just as refugees, but also as immigrants, tourists, and business travelers. I remember he had a very dark theory of human migration in relationship to technology and globalization. I also vaguely remember him talking about the need for migration to another planet.

GQ: The questions of migration and the complexity of the world involve various ways of thinking and perspectives. It was your suggestion to involve many different types of knowledges, including philosophers, artists, statisticians, and anthropologists. You worked closely with architect-artist Laura Kurgan, statistician-artist Mark Hansen, artist-designer Ben Rubin, as well as with the Fondation Cartier, and French specialists François Gemenne, Bruce Albert, and François-Michel Le Tourneau. How did *EXIT* take form?

ED: We knew we wanted to make two media-oriented pieces in two galleries. One of them was with Ben Rubin, a collaborator on previous works. This was a cross-section of archival news footage, photographs, and documentaries about global migration on a given day. The imagery was displayed on forty-eight monitors hanging from the gallery ceiling. The clips were choreographed according to visual cues, such as color, motion, speed, or image composition, with groups of related images flocking and flowing across the viewing field. The multiscreen composition could be viewed in its entirety, as an ensemble, or on single monitors as individual stories. Over the course of the piece, patterns would emerge on screen suggesting links between various global events. It was an aesthetic re-framing of the media's coverage of global migrations.

The second piece was also about global migration, but using data visualization as the sole medium. First, I invited Laura Kurgan. She was a colleague and I was inspired by her innovative mapping projects—at the time, she was working on a seminal piece about the effects of incarceration on inner cities. She became the prime collaborator on content. Mark Hansen was brought onboard as a statistician and data miner, though he is also an artist. He was politically oriented, as was Laura, so it made for a great core team. Then François Gemenne came in as a general resource, while Bruce Albert and François-Michel Le Tourneau, specialists in anthropology and geography, were invited by Hervé to develop a particular story on endangered languages and deforestation. In our studio, Robert Gerard Pietrusko, an architect with a strong digital orientation, worked with Laura and me on the transformation of data into motion, which generated the maps. Bobby wrote all the code and was part of the creative and content-generating team. Stewart Smith helped us implement a graphic strategy. Along with a small group of architects in my studio, the entire collaborative team worked to generate the project over the next year. It was intense.

GQ: *EXIT* is an innovation in terms of data visualization and its use in the art world. It is a contemporary visual strategy, showing data from a human perspective, accessible and easily understandable by the public. How did you develop its technology?

ED: The more conventional method of telling heartfelt stories of human suffering and displacement is through film, photography, and other time-based media. We wanted to try an alternative approach. We started by interrogating the notion of "home." Sometimes you leave home to find work, sometimes because you've been involuntarily displaced. If you've been displaced, you're either an internally displaced person (IDP) or a refugee. So the challenge was to tell these difficult human stories using dispassionate information culled from the most reliable data sources, while creating an emotional impact over approximately forty-five minutes.

Using animated data visualization to tell poignant stories was recently possible with open source creative software designed as drawing tools. We repurposed it for data visualization. We're all familiar with data visualization, from the most primitive maps to modern infographics. They're designed to make a point but are usually still and didactic. Animating the information in a powerful yet unsentimental way was a difficult task. Oddly enough, our first point of reference was the IBM Selectric typewriter. It had an unusual golf ball-like typing mechanism—the "typeball"—that rotated to deposit text on a page. From the typist's point of view, the individual characters on the typeball appeared backwards. So we came up with the idea of a backwards globe that would spin around a circular room and digitally print the information—maps made out of pixels unrolled on the surrounding wall. It created a dual condition where you're simultaneously on the outside of the globe, and also inside of it because the maps are printed all around you. The globe was the lynchpin of the project.

We also had to decide how to create a meaningful narrative. Pixels were the building blocks of the piece, and we moved them around our digital canvas to animate the maps. We developed algorithms, which assigned the quantity and location of the pixels, and the maps would essentially build themselves once we had sufficient data to tell each individual story. This effect allowed us to generate landmasses with geocoded data rather than drawing political or geographic boundaries. We incorporated very minimal texts only where we felt the narrative needed more context. In other words, we let the processed and interpreted data do the storytelling.

GQ: How did you conceive the installation's architecture?

ED: Rather than looking at the globe from space, like the "Blue Marble" image of Earth, we wanted to make the experience immersive. So we created this circular projection space where maps were unfurled in 360 degrees around the audience. The maps were then animated to dynamically show different datasets. You can continuously spin in the space to track the globe or pixels migrating from place to place. But beyond the visually immersive quality of the installation, we realized that without sound the piece wouldn't have the emotional effect we wanted. We asked Hans-Christoph Steiner to collaborate on the spatialized sound. One of the great sounds was the globe, which generates an intense rumble that you can feel in your chest. This was inspired by the boulder scene in the Indiana Jones movie *Raiders of the Lost Ark*. But the sound was electronic. Also, whenever the globe spins to deposit digital information and text, there is a deep clicking sound that we pulled directly from the IBM Selectric typewriter.

GQ: *EXIT* was created in 2008 and fully updated to coincide with COP21, the United Nations Climate Change Conference held in Paris in 2015. Following this presentation, between 2017 and 2018, it was shown in Australia, China, and Chile, as part of climate-related events. How do you think the impact on the public, or their reaction, has changed from the first iteration until today?

ED: The Fondation Cartier is unique. I can't think of any comparable arts institution that would have commissioned a project like *EXIT*. It was arguably more of a geography or political science research project than an art installation, and in 2008, it was truly novel to animate data in this fashion. The bet paid off: *EXIT* was a hit with the public. There was a long line outside the building for the entire run of the show because everyone wanted to see the story from beginning to end—all forty-five minutes—and there was limited space. And it wasn't just academics and experts who were lining up to see the show—there was the art crowd, students, kids, and their parents. It interested a true cross section of the public.

Since the Fondation Cartier is an acclaimed venue, *EXIT* was able to get widespread exposure and travel the world. When the piece was shown in Copenhagen for COP15 and then in Paris for COP21, it gained a particular urgency in the context of global climate change negotiations. After six years, for COP21, *EXIT* was updated to reflect more recent political and environmental crises, including the Syrian civil war. Since then, the rate of migration has only continued to accelerate, and global politics have become increasingly volatile. In many ways, people are responding to *EXIT* with a greater sense of gravity.

This is why we want to show the piece where it will have the most impact. When we showed a version of *EXIT* at COP21, policy makers responded with a great deal of interest. They said that typically, they see various data visualizations—such as flood displacement, wartime migration, economic emigration—but in isolation from one another. Because we assembled the data across topics, policy makers could see new connections between various issues, like weather and economics.

GQ: More than ten years have passed since the creation of *EXIT*. If you were starting the project today, what would you do differently? Make it bigger? Tackle different subjects?

ED: The last topic in *EXIT*, *Speechless and Deforestation*, was added after all the other chapters were completely composed. Bruce Albert and François-Michel Le Tourneau played a crucial role in its elaboration and Laura mobilized much of the research. The Fondation Cartier also collected data on the endangered languages from the UNESCO in Paris. There are 6,700 languages in danger of extinction by the year 2100. Fundamentally, the loss of language has to do with economic and environmental factors. We focused on desertification and deforestation, which are major culprits, but I think we could have done a deeper dive by looking at other root causes, such as overfishing and resource extraction. The latter was the subject of a subsequent collaboration between Laura, Bobby, and myself called *In Plain Sight* at the 2018 Venice Architecture Biennale. Overall though, I wouldn't approach the work any differently.

GQ: *EXIT* is part of the Fondation Cartier's Collection, which also includes other works dealing with visualization of data. For example, in *The Great Animal Orchestra* by bioacoustician Bernie Krause and the studio United Visual Artists, the sounds of nature are made visible, bringing the degradation of ecosystems into focus. Do you think that such works can help develop a shared approach to world problems?

ED: Bernie Krause's piece is brilliant. In *The Great Animal Orchestra*, Bernie recorded animal sounds in the same spot several years apart, and then visualized their sound signatures. It is both beautiful and devastating, because you are able to hear and see the absence of animal tonalities in the more recent recordings—clear evidence of the degradation of natural habitats. This is an incredibly powerful tool for environmental advocacy. What I think both *EXIT* and *The Great Animal Orchestra* have in common is the effective reworking of data to provoke an emotional response in the viewer. In our case, when you see 1,000 pixels that stand for 10,000 displaced people, it's one degree less abstract than numerals, and that's why a simple point or pixel can carry such emotional weight.

Interview held in April 2019

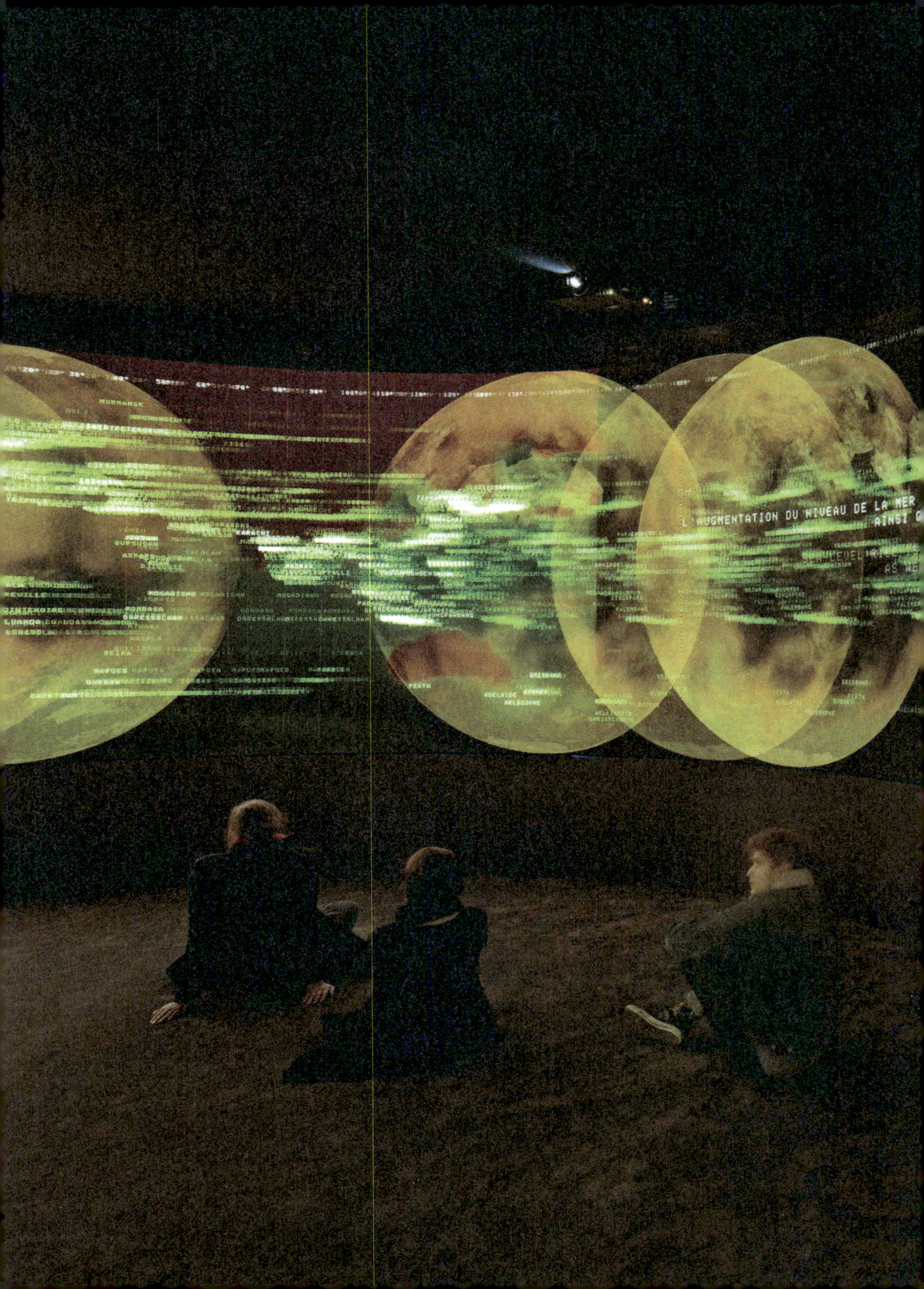
L'AUGMENTATION DU NIVEAU DE LA MER

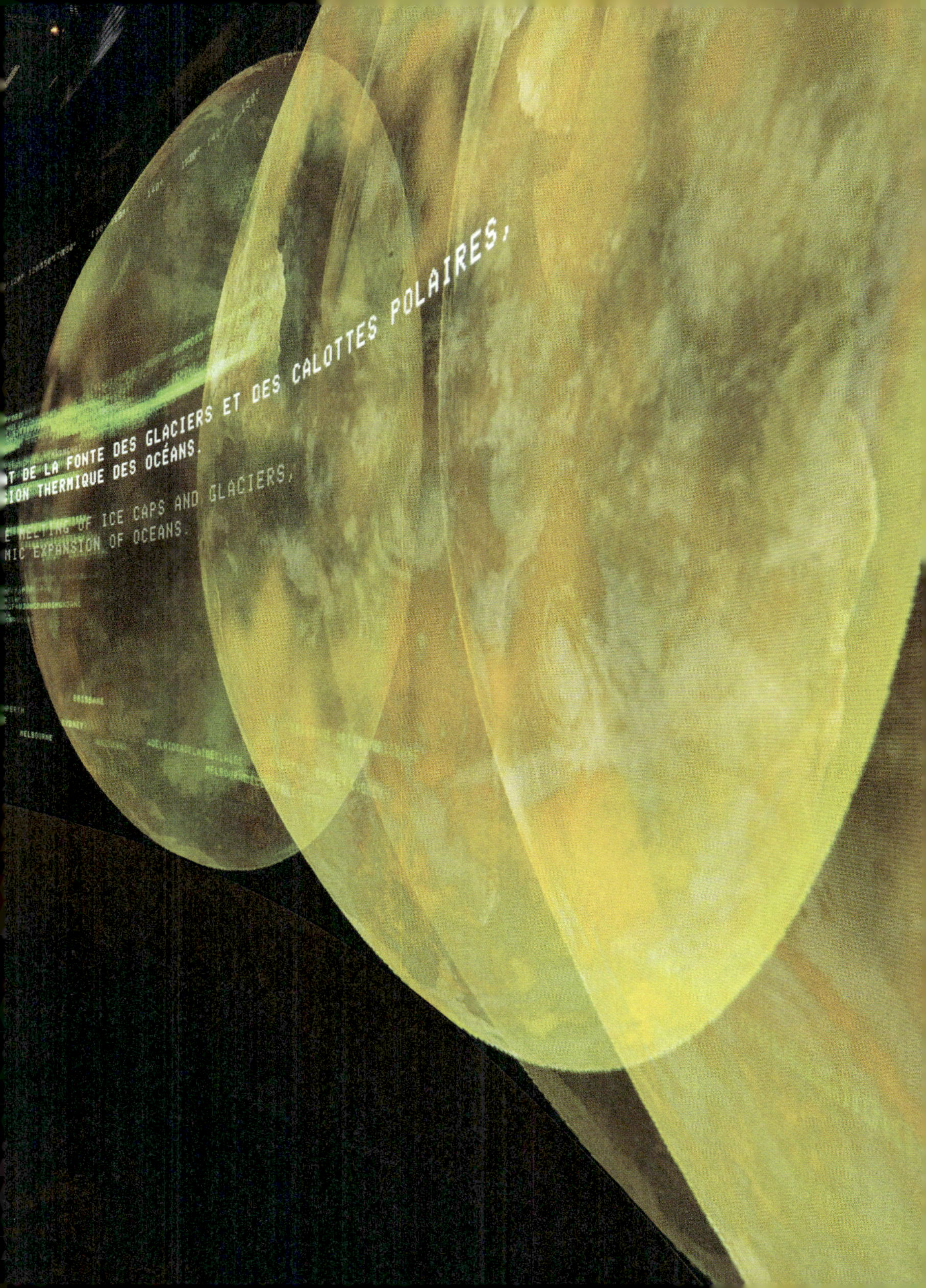
T DE LA FONTE DES GLACIERS ET DES CALOTTES POLAIRES,
ION THERMIQUE DES OCÉANS.
E MELTING OF ICE CAPS AND GLACIERS,
MIC EXPANSION OF OCEANS.
BRISBANE
PERTH
SYDNEY
MELBOURNE

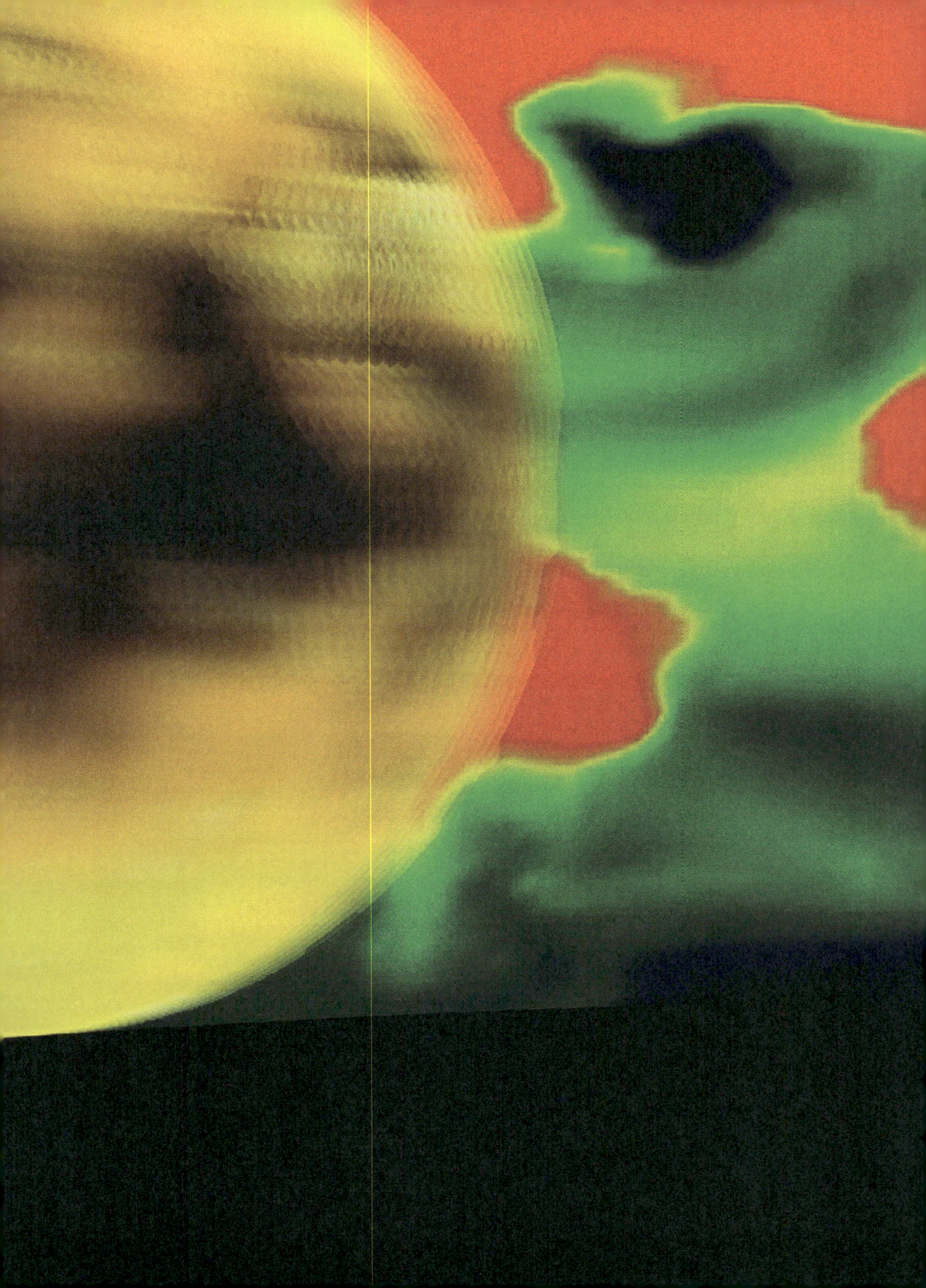

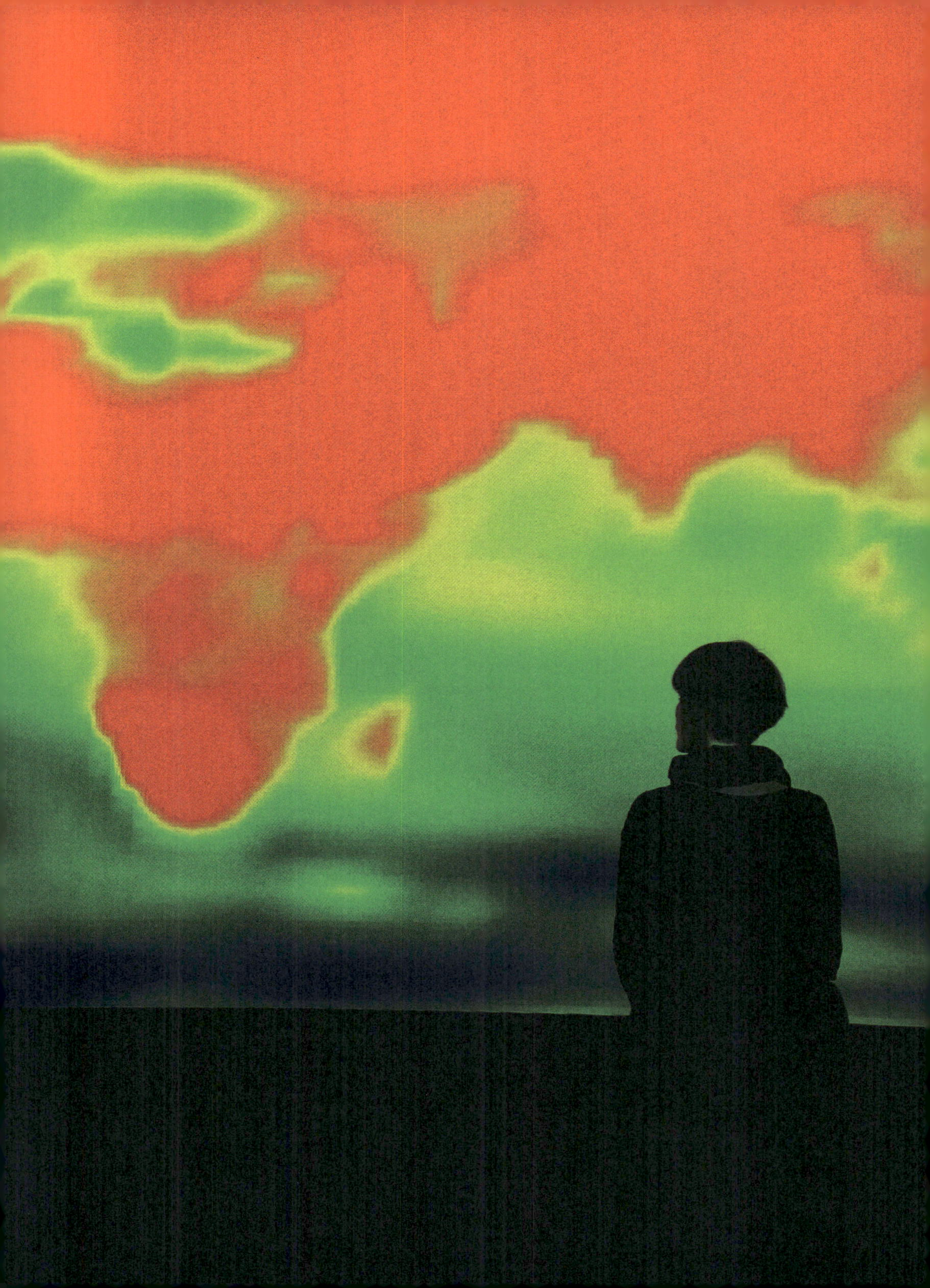

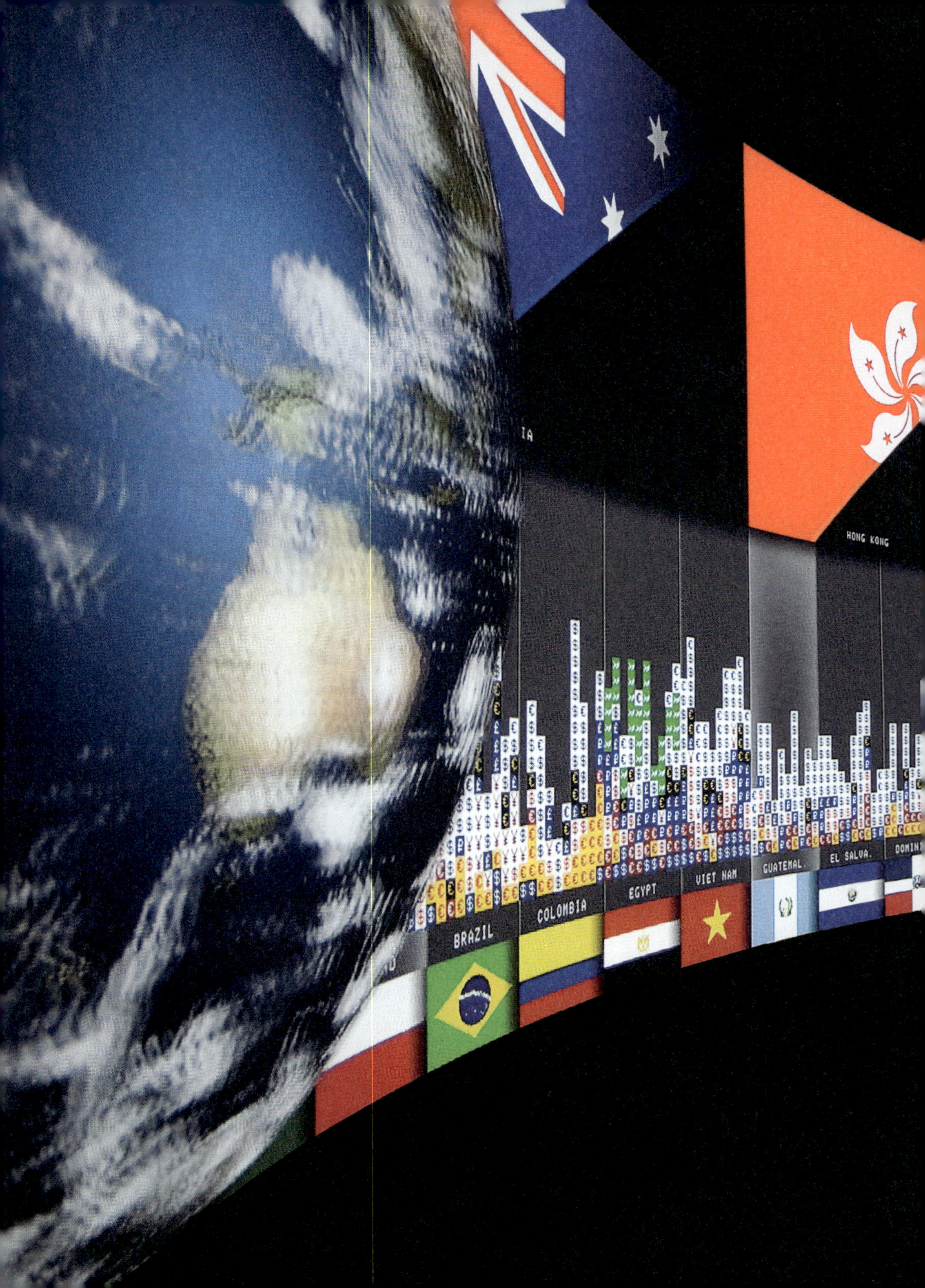
HONG KONG
BRAZIL
COLOMBIA
EGYPT
VIET NAM
GUATEMAL.
EL SALVA.

About *EXIT*

by Elizabeth Diller,
Laura Kurgan, and Mark Hansen

Paul Virilio's prompt to us for the 2008 exhibition *Native Land, Stop Eject* was to respond spatially to his discourse on human migration and its root causes. Commissioned at a time when human migration flows had increased to an unprecedented scale, our intent with *EXIT* was to quantify, interpret, and display this global trend as well as its underlying causes. We worked with Paul Virilio, François Gemenne, and the curatorial team at the Fondation Cartier to create this work.

The project examines stationary people who are forced to migrate against their will, and migratory people who are restricted, even detained, in their movements. While the energies behind this flow of people are different and often contradictory, we have gathered the data into three broad categories: political, economic, and environmental. We have also focused on tracing and registering the complex forces that shape the pathways of human mobility. They are twofold at least: people leave or are driven away from the places they live, but they are also attracted to or pulled by new places. This push/pull dynamic is at the heart of *EXIT*.

In the immersive environment of a circular projection, the installation surrounds its viewers with the repetitive motion of a globe that circles the room as it spins; with each orbit, the globe writes and rewrites translations of data of human migration into maps, texts, and trajectories. One orbit takes forty-five seconds.

EXIT comprises six scenes, focusing on population shift, remittances, political refugees, natural disasters, sea-level rise, and speechless and deforestation. Each scene first begins with a world view, then zooms in to specific locations with data made tangible, allowing the viewer to focus on a particular slice of the Earth.

The piece is an experiment in both storytelling and expanding the potential of data visualization. The landmasses in the maps are not illustrated but rather built from pixels generated by data collected from various sources. The data is geocoded, processed through a programming language, and interpreted visually. We wanted to make palpable, and even emotive, the drama around the uprooting of people from their homes using only data—without resorting to the crutch of conventional narrative media such as film, photography, or words. *EXIT* is an experiment in abstraction.

EXIT converges geographical, economic, environmental, and political data that are typically seen in isolation. In doing so, it exposes relations that are otherwise not visible. The information we use was collected from over one hundred sources including international organizations, NGOs, and research centers. Sourcing objective information was a challenge. Statistics documenting population shifts are not always neutral and existing datasets are decentralized and incomplete. While mindful of the work each organization had undertaken to produce the data, we intentionally re-functioned it. The organizations have not been asked to vouch for or endorse the map content of the exhibition.

The 2015 update of *EXIT* coincided with the pivotal COP21, Paris-based United Nations Climate Change Conference. It revealed a major increase in the data documenting human migrations since the first iteration of the work in 2008. Since the update, the pace of human migration has continued to intensify. The current political instability around the world and the asylum crisis makes *EXIT* timelier and more relevant now than when we began. We hope to expand the audience of *EXIT* in the foreseeable future.

New York, May 2019

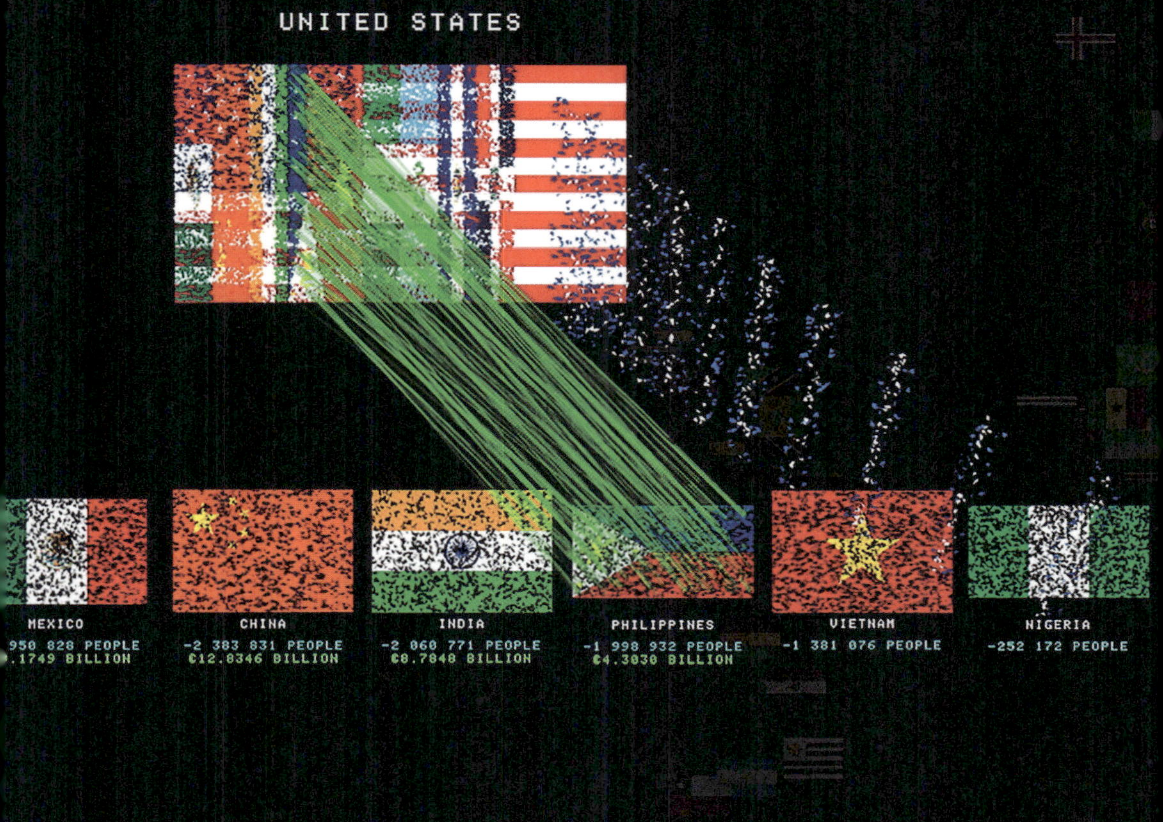

UNITED STATES
MEXICO
950 828 PEOPLE
.1749 BILLION
CHINA
-2 383 831 PEOPLE
€12.8346 BILLION
INDIA
-2 060 771 PEOPLE
€8.7848 BILLION
PHILIPPINES
-1 998 932 PEOPLE
€4.3030 BILLION
VIETNAM
-1 381 076 PEOPLE
NIGERIA
-252 172 PEOPLE

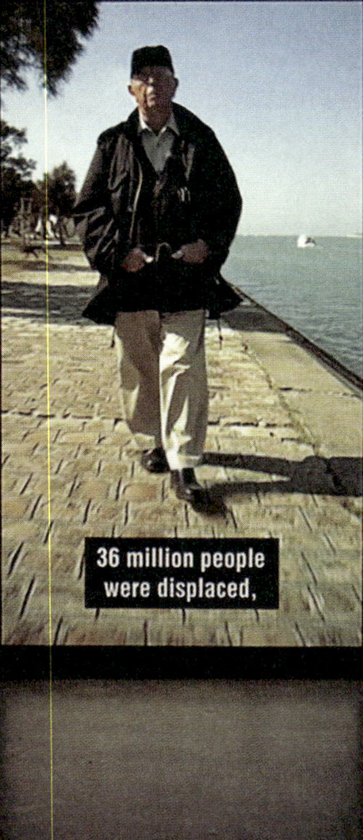

36 million people
were displaced,

EXIT
Foreword

by Paul Virilio

Latest News:
In 2008, 36 million people were displaced, due to climate, natural disasters, or conflicts. The twenty-first century will be the century of mass migrations. A billion people in the next fifty years is the figure predicted. A billion people will move. The whole world situation will be disrupted. Disrupted by the crisis in localization. The old societies were connected to a territory, a Native Land. Today they're adrift due to the delocalization of jobs and never-ending conflicts. There is also, clearly, the major issue of climate: the disappearance of archipelagoes, submersion of coastlines. This means all of history is on the move again. All of history is taking to the road. A billion people moving over half a century. That's never been seen before. All this calls into question, what? Sedentariness, the city, the fact of being here and not elsewhere, the fact of being settled in a region, in a nation. Immigrants are just the forerunners of the great traceability to come. Identity means you are connected to a place. Traceability means you go with the flow, you go on a never-ending journey. Today the sedentary person is at home everywhere, thanks to telecommunications, to interactivity. The nomad is nowhere at home, except in transit camps, here and there. So, the question for us is: how will we cope with this perpetual motion, the perpetual motion of history in motion? Not the history of great invasions anymore, or of what I'd call conflict-based displacements, but the

← Introduction to the installation by Paul Virilio

history of climate change, where the weather matters more than geography. As if aeropolitics were about to submerge geopolitics. Meaning, the development of space, of land. It's almost as though the sky, and the clouds in it and the pollution of it, were making their entry into history. Not the history of the seasons, summer, autumn, winter, but of population flows, of zones now uninhabitable for reasons that aren't just to do with desertification, but with disappearance, with submersion of land. This is the future.

La Rochelle, 2008

EXIT
The Maps

by Diller Scofidio + Renfro,
Mark Hansen, Laura Kurgan,
and Ben Rubin, in collaboration with
Robert Gerard Pietrusko and Stewart Smith

Global populations are unstable and on the move. Unprecedented numbers of migrants are leaving their home countries for political, economic, and environmental reasons. *EXIT* was created to quantify and display this increasingly urgent global condition.

The presentation is divided into six narratives: *Population Shifts: Cities*; *Remittances: Sending Money Home*; *Political Refugees and Forced Migration*; *Natural Disasters*; *Rising Seas, Sinking Cities*; and *Speechless and Deforestation*. The following pages present each of these narratives and show selected stills from the installation.

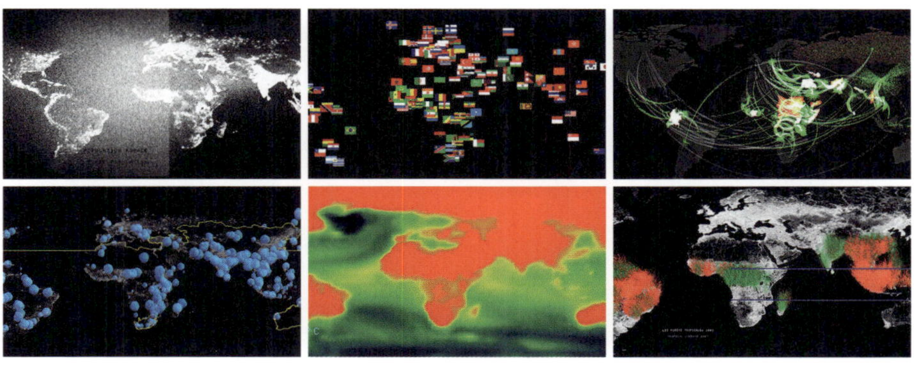

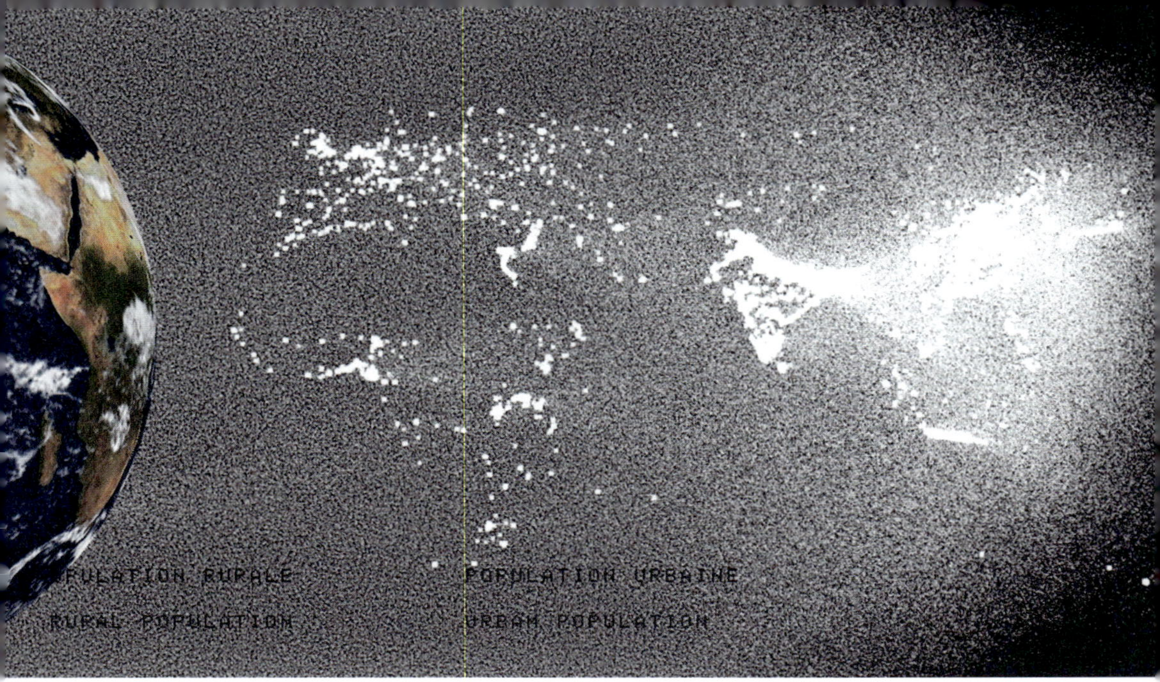

Population Shifts: Cities

As of 2007, the population shift to urban areas equaled that of rural areas worldwide. The first map shows this shift: each pixel of the map represents one thousand people, and the pixel distribution between urban and rural areas is the same. The more densely pixels are packed, the more brightly they shine.

In order to show population change over time, the data are subsequently visualized as a series of straight lines drawn across the globe at specific latitudes that transform into a series of graphs. The x-axis displays longitude and latitude, and the y-axis is distorted to show decline and growth in population.

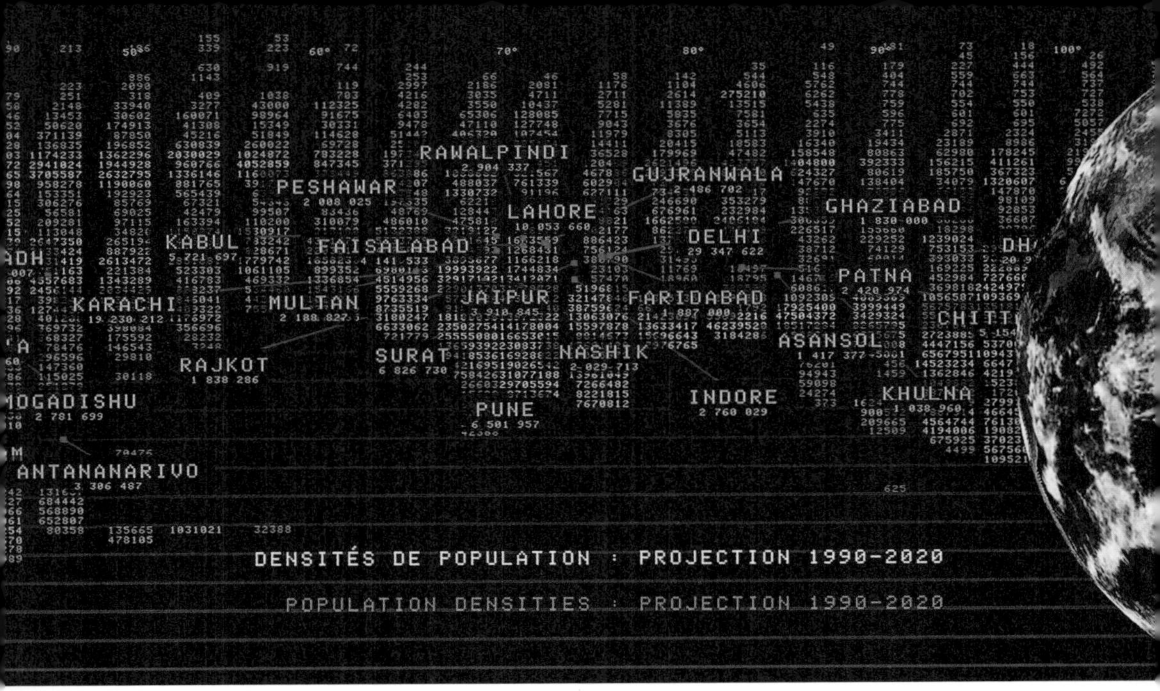

Finally, the globe's longitude stretches to a 360° projection in which each pixel is rendered as an animated counter. The pixels count goes up or down according to population change as recorded by census data. The fifty fastest growing cities in the world with over one million people in 2015 come into focus, with forty-eight in the Global South and two in the North.

Data sources: Gridded Population of the World, version 3 (GPWv3) and version 4 (GPWv4): Center for International Earth Science Information Network (CIESIN), Columbia University; International Food Policy Research Institute (IFPRI); The World Bank; Centro Internacional de Agricultura Tropical (CIAT), 2015 / The world's fastest growing cities and urban areas from 2006 to 2020: City Mayors, Statistics

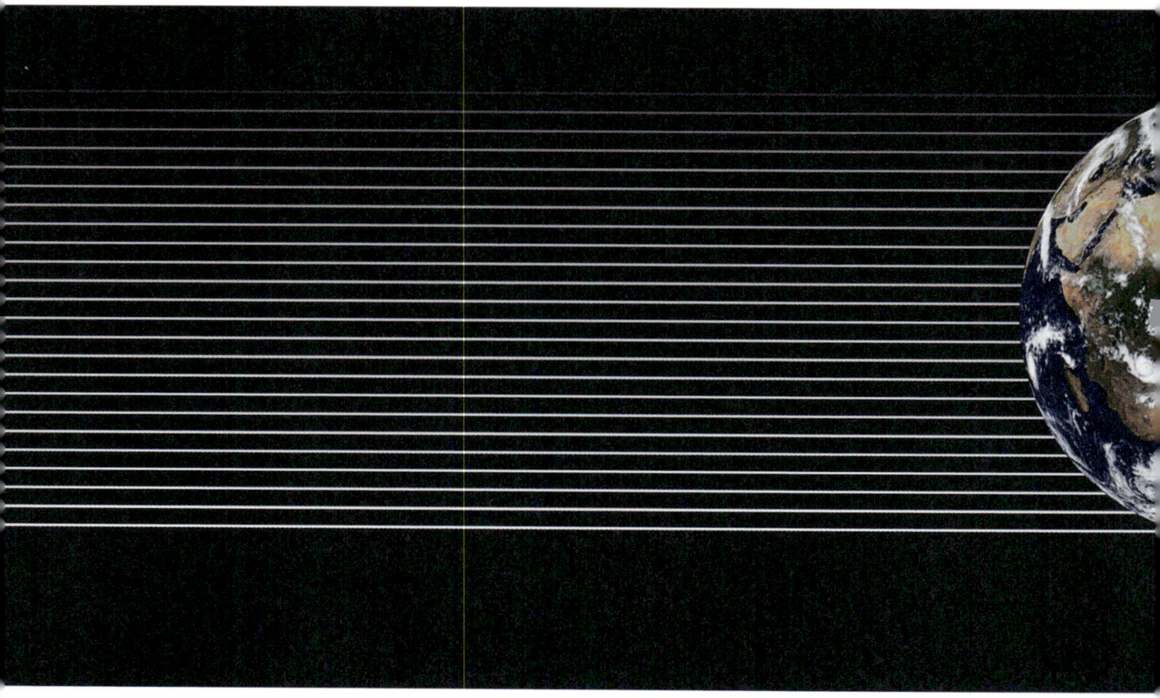

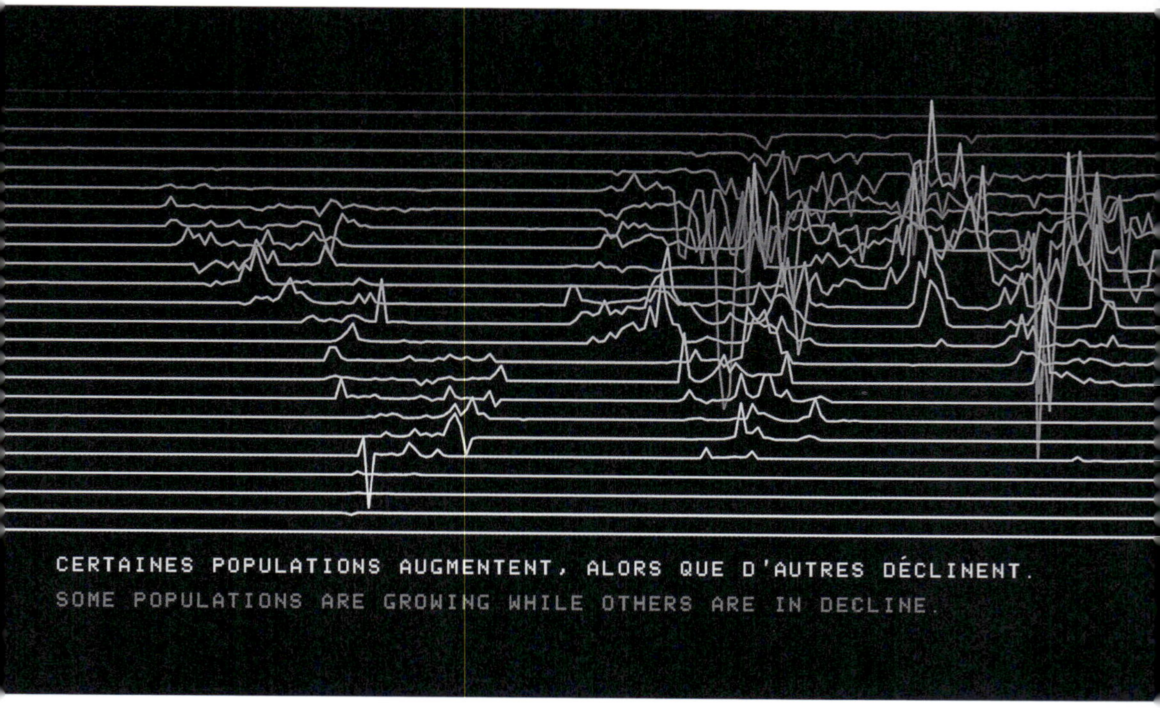

CERTAINES POPULATIONS AUGMENTENT, ALORS QUE D'AUTRES DÉCLINENT.
SOME POPULATIONS ARE GROWING WHILE OTHERS ARE IN DECLINE.

Map *Population Shifts: Cities* by Diller Scofidio + Renfro, Mark Hansen, Laura Kurgan, and Ben Rubin, in collaboration with Robert Gerard Pietrusko and Stewart Smith

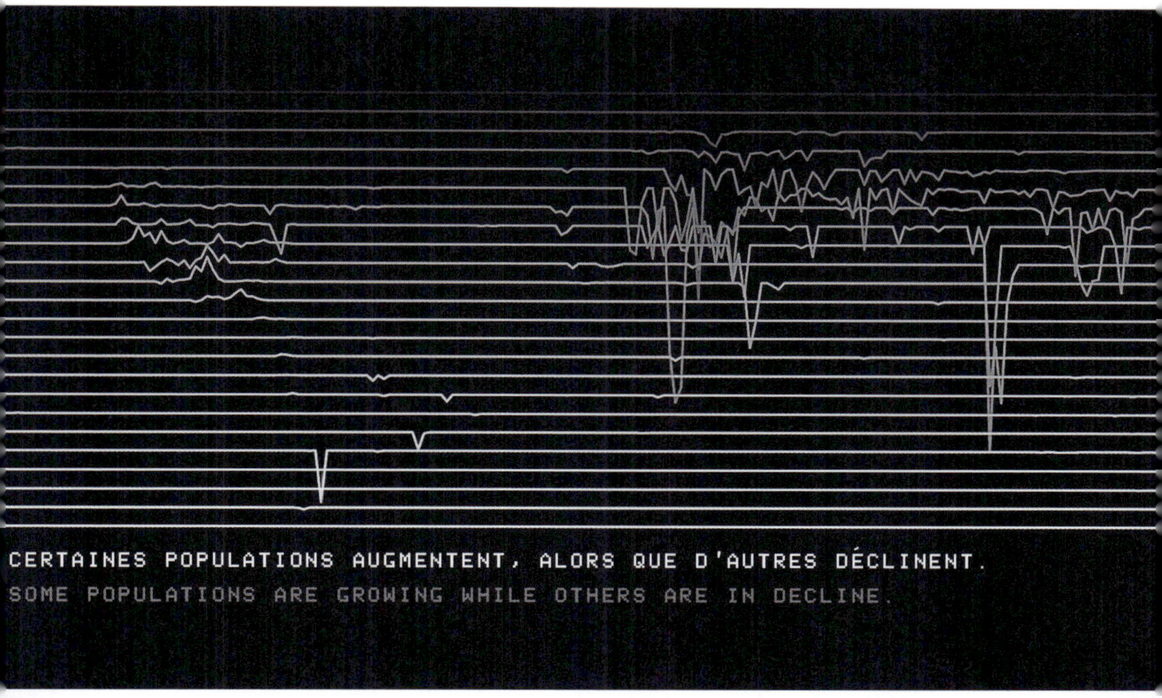

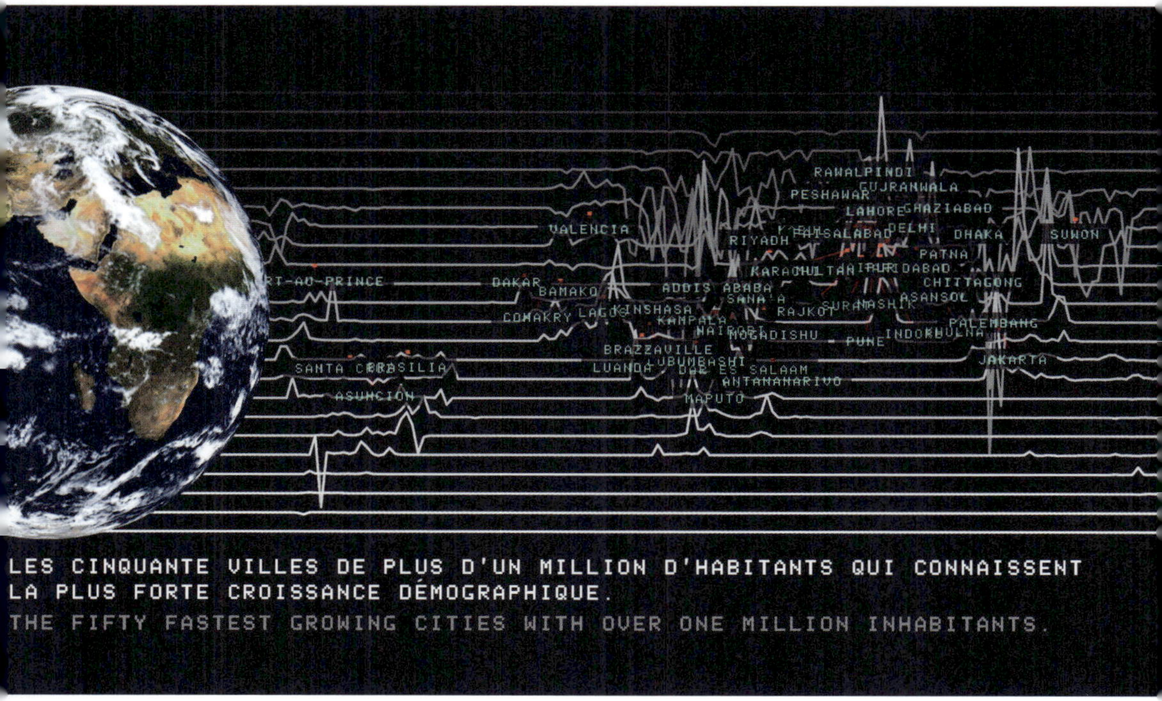

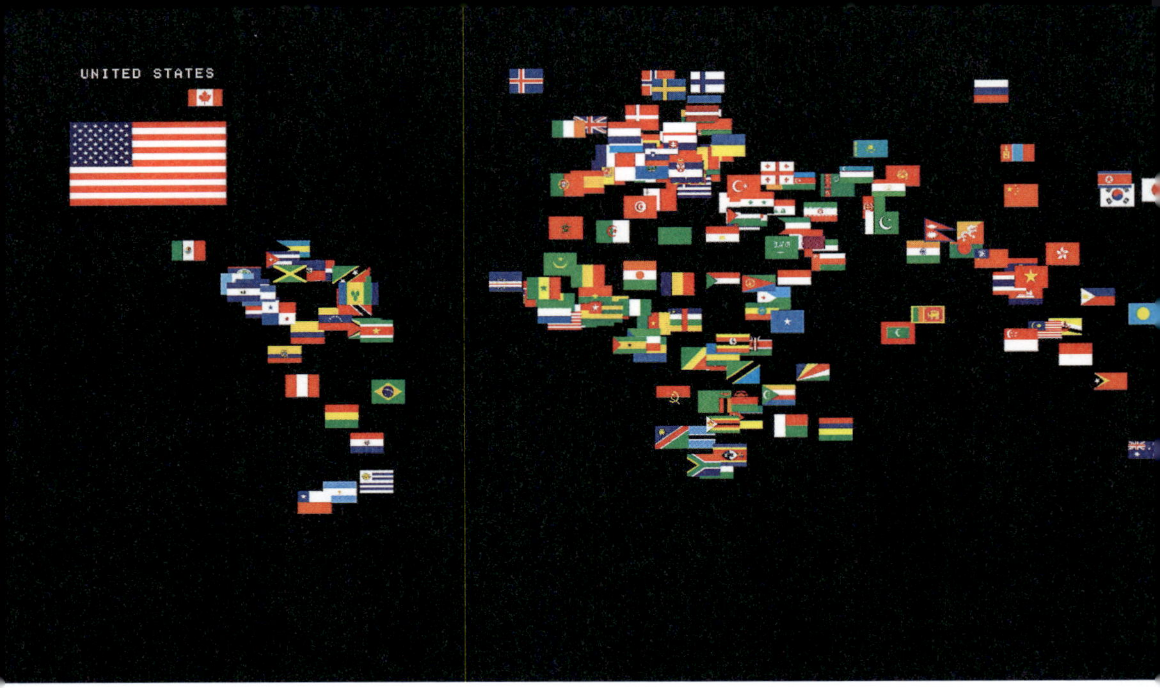

Remittances: Sending Money Home

Remittances comprise an informal economic network that plays a crucial role in the developing world. Remittances from migrants are often the primary source of foreign investment in developing countries. In 2014, migrants sent more than 389 billion euros to developing countries. In these countries, remittances exceed foreign aid by 3 to 1.

To visualize these transnational networks, each country is represented as a flag on the map. When displaying data about a "home" country, its flag is enlarged and people move to their "host" countries. Eventually, each nation is resized in its new location in proportion to the number of people who have immigrated. To visualize remittance, the direction of movement on the map is reversed and money flows back home through thin lines connecting the sending and receiving nations. The flags appear to lose pixels and become threadbare in proportion to the loss of people or funds. Data shows that 15 percent of countries worldwide account for 80 percent of the immigrant inflow and 90 percent of the remittance outflow.

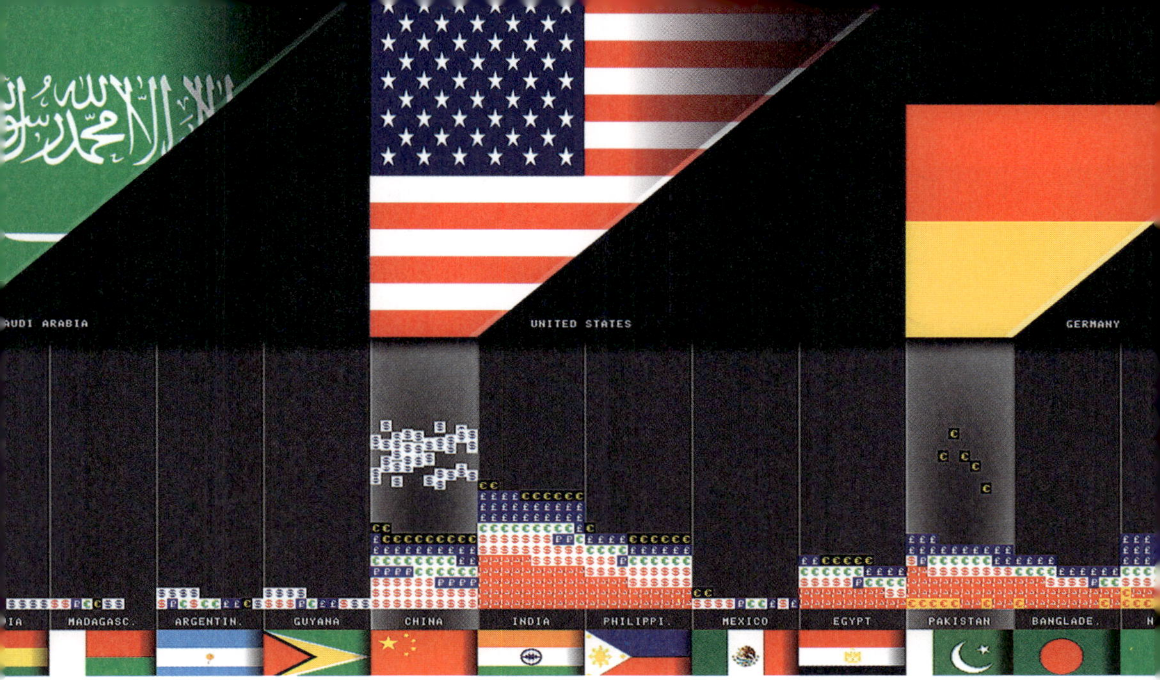

To underscore the relationships between the home and host countries, the data is sifted, reassembled, and sorted into a container surrounding the viewer. A chart appears, showing the sums of remittances received by "home" country in relation to its GDP and foreign aid. Seventy developing countries receive 60 percent of global remittances from migrants living in twenty host nations.

Data sources: Global Migrant Origin Database (updated March 2007): The Development Research Centre on Migration, Globalisation and Poverty (Migration DRC), University of Sussex / Bilateral migration matrix and Bilateral remittance estimates (using migrant stocks, destination country incomes, and source country incomes): data associated with World Bank Working Paper No. 102 "South-South Migration and Remittances" / Sending Money Home: Worldwide Remittance flows to developing countries: The International Fund for Agricultural Development (IFAD) / Statistical Annex from the 2007 Development Co-operation Report, Development Co-operation Directorate (DCD-DAC), Organisation for Economic Co-operation and Development (OECD) / World Economic and Financial Surveys, World Economic Outlook Database (April 2008 Edition), International Monetary Fund (IMF) / WEO Groups and Aggregates Information, World Economic and Financial Surveys, World Economic Outlook Database (April 2008 Edition)

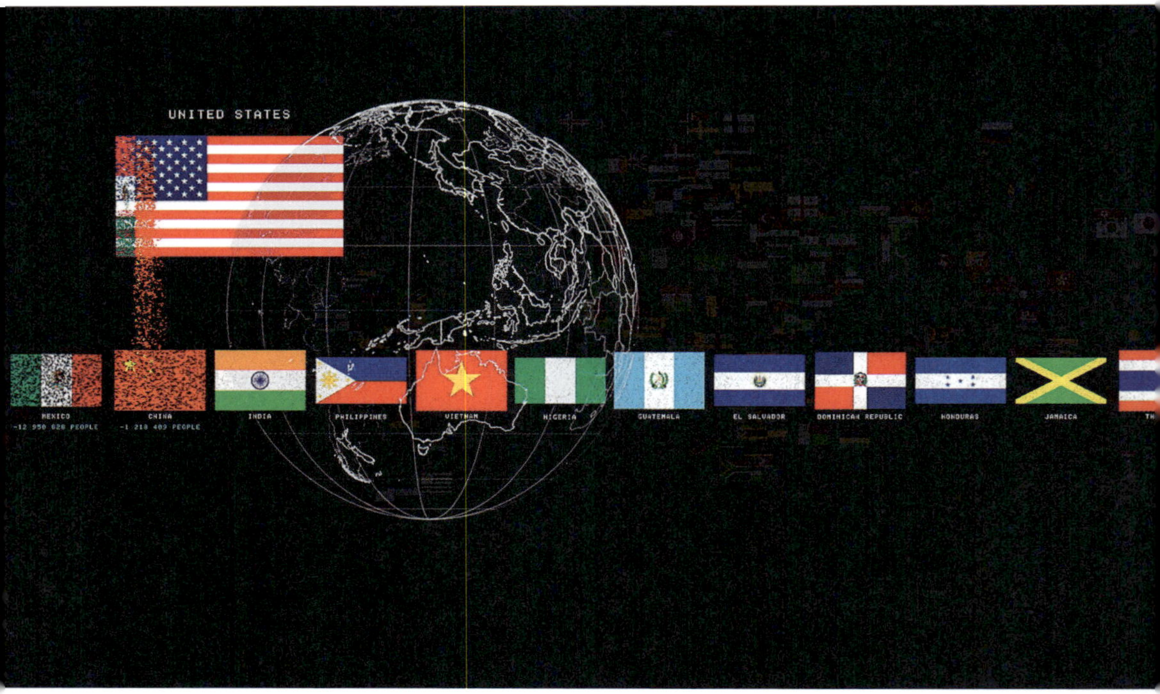
UNITED STATES
MEXICO
CHINA
INDIA
PHILIPPINES
VIETNAM
NIGERIA
GUATEMALA
EL SALVADOR
DOMINICAN REPUBLIC
HONDURAS
JAMAICA

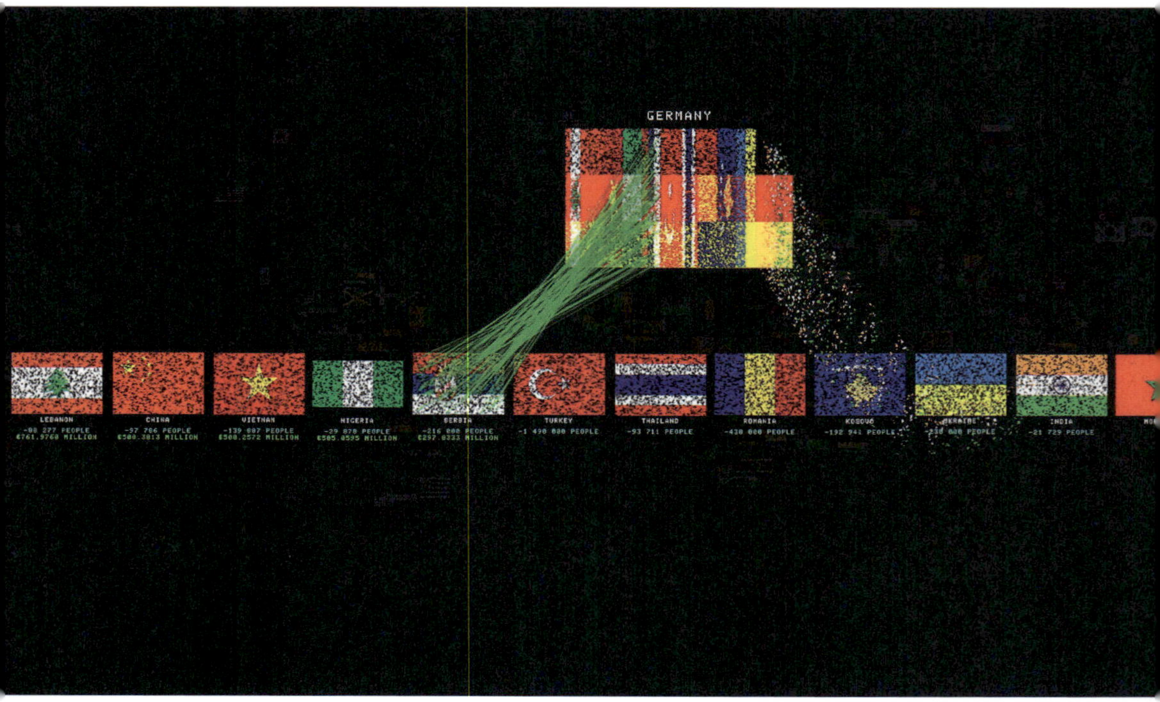
GERMANY
LEBANON
CHINA
VIETNAM
NIGERIA
SERBIA
TURKEY
THAILAND
ROMANIA
KOSOVO
INDIA

Map *Remittances: Sending Money Home* by Diller Scofidio + Renfro, Mark Hansen, Laura Kurgan, and Ben Rubin, in collaboration with Robert Gerard Pietrusko and Stewart Smith

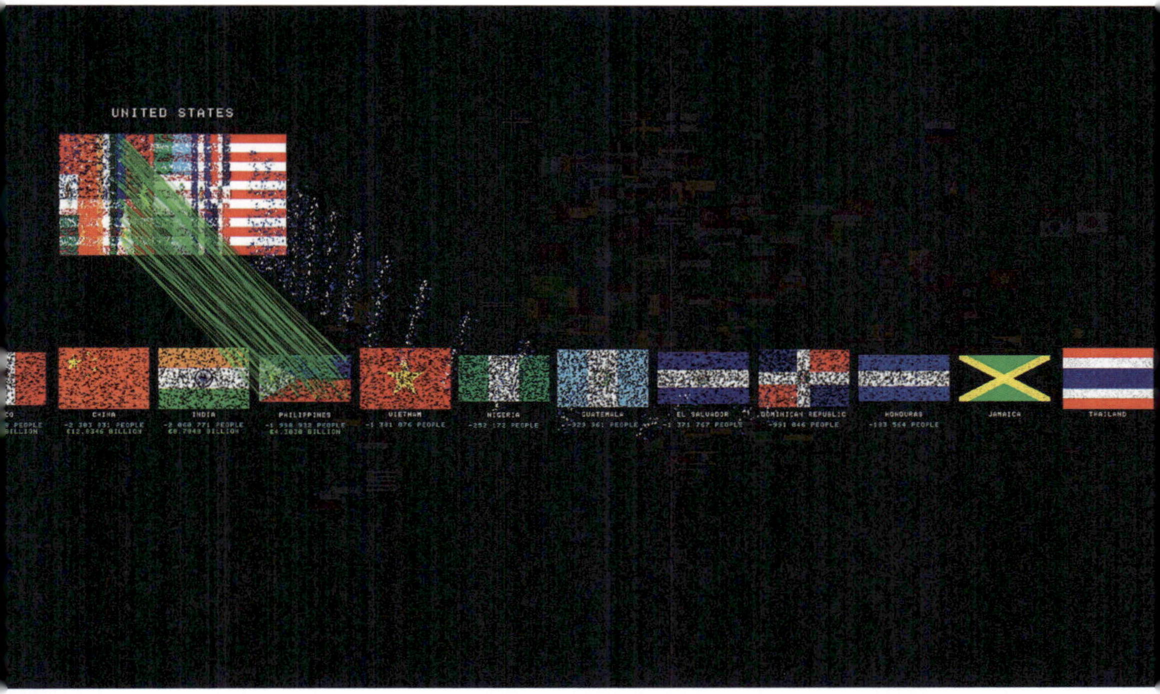

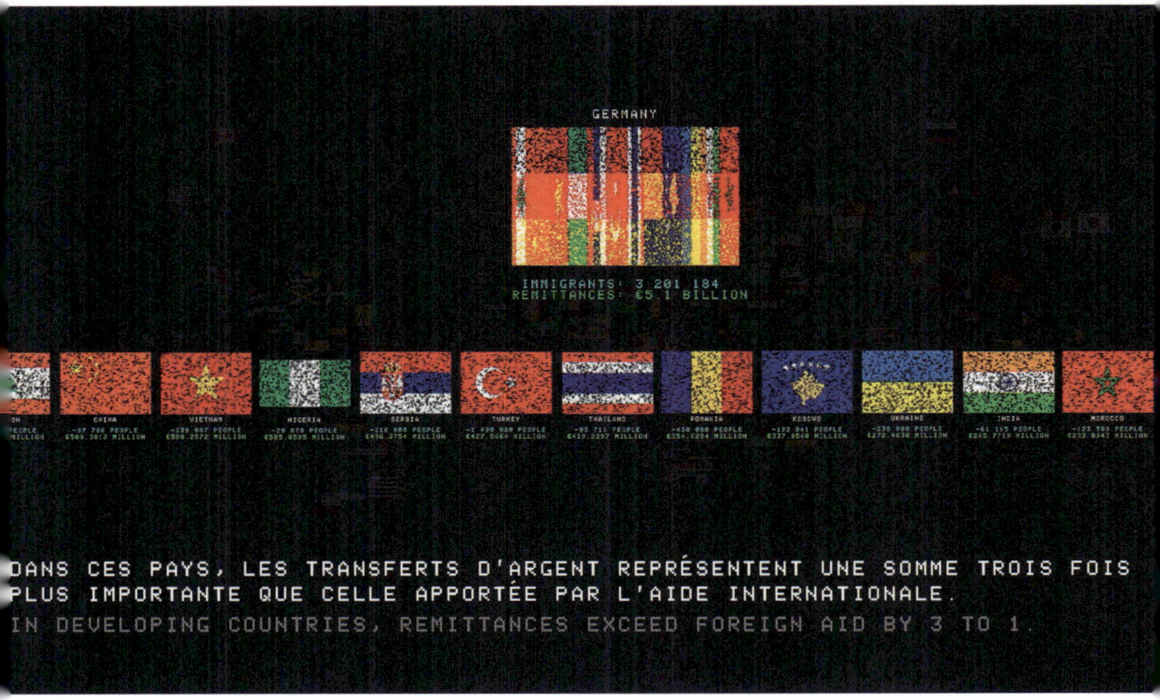

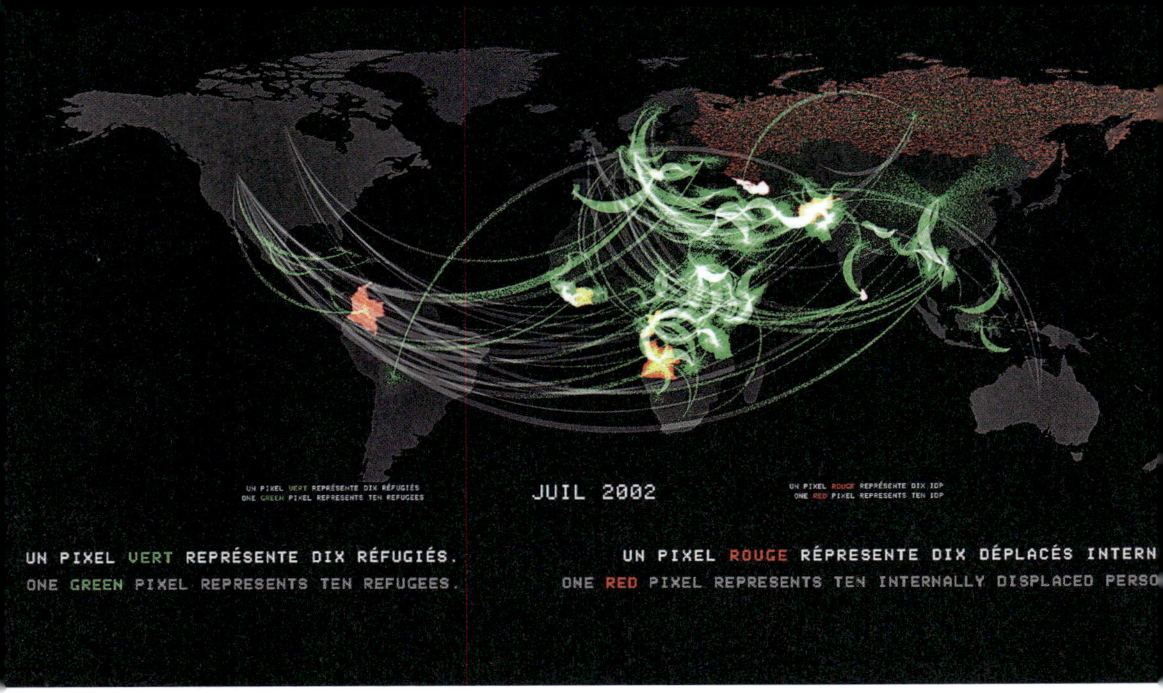

Political Refugees and Forced Migration

While mobility is often a metaphor for freedom, it is sometimes a tragic necessity—the threats faced by people who are otherwise attached to their land but forced to move, or perils faced by those who want to move and find their paths largely predetermined or simply blocked. The journeys made by forced migrants, whether they are refugees, asylum seekers, or internally displaced people (IDP) reveal the obstacles they meet along the way: refused asylum, turned back at the border, detained, or worse.

This map shows the continuous movement of people forced to migrate away from their homes because of war, persecution, and violence. Refugees are displaced outside of their country, while IDPs are displaced within their own country. Green pixels represent refugees and red pixels represent IDPs. As of 2015, 57.5 million people were forcibly displaced worldwide, including 19.5 million refugees and 38 million IDPs. It was the highest number since the end of World War II.

Drawing on data from United Nations High Commissioner for Refugees (UNHCR), one pixel moving across the screen represents

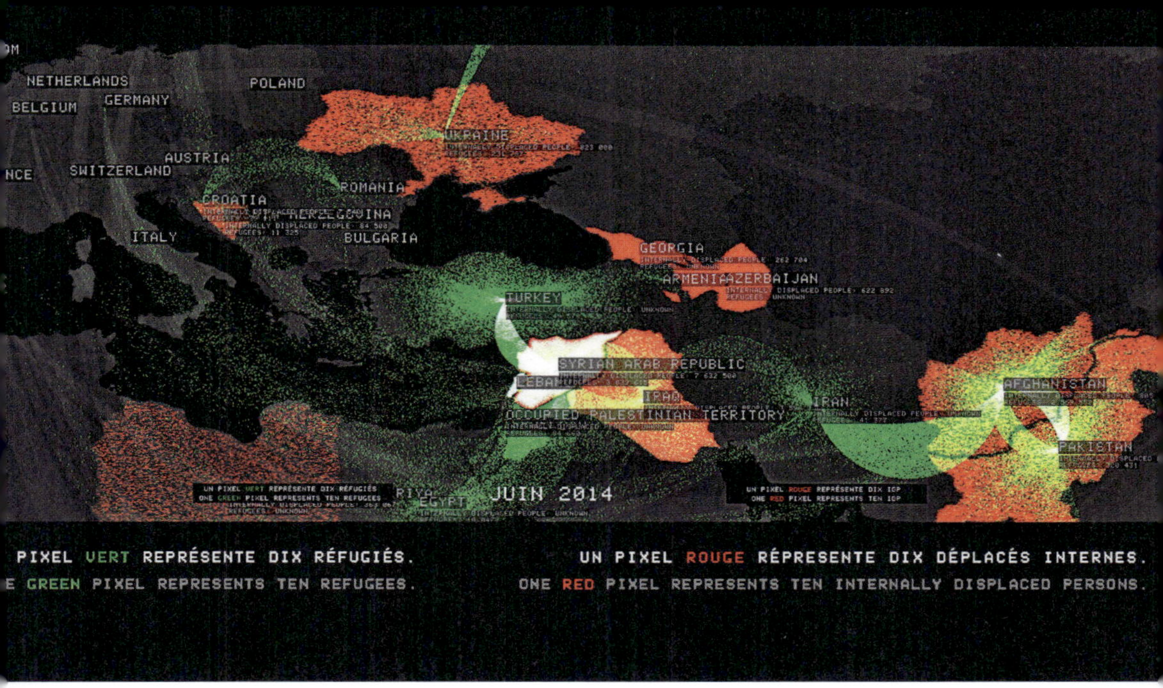

ten people in the database. The pixels draw paths from one country's center point to the next, and are sized according to the numbers of people displaced in a like manner. Swarms of pixels move across the screen, which signify people leaving certain places to seek refuge in others. All of the movement slowly traces a map, locating refugees, asylum seekers, and IDPs.

Data sources: United Nations High Commissioner for Refugees (UNHCR), Online Statistical Population Database (scraped August 2015) **/** Historical Maps, Field Information and Coordination Support Section, Division of operational Services, UNHCR **/** Vector Map Level 0 (VMap), Transportation layer, Roads and Railroads **/** Digital Chart of the World Server, Penn State University Libraries **/** Digital Aeronautical Fight Information File (DAFIF), a product of the National Imagery and Mapping Agency (NIMA) of the United States Department of Defense (DOD) **/** Complete Files of Geographic Names for Geopolitical Areas from The GEOnet Names Server, National Geospatial-Intelligence Agency **/** World Aeronautical Database **/** Refugees Stories: Refugees International; International Rescue Committee; US Committee for Refugees and Immigrants; Middle East Institute; Doctors Without Borders; Church World Service; Blog: Rwanda Survivors

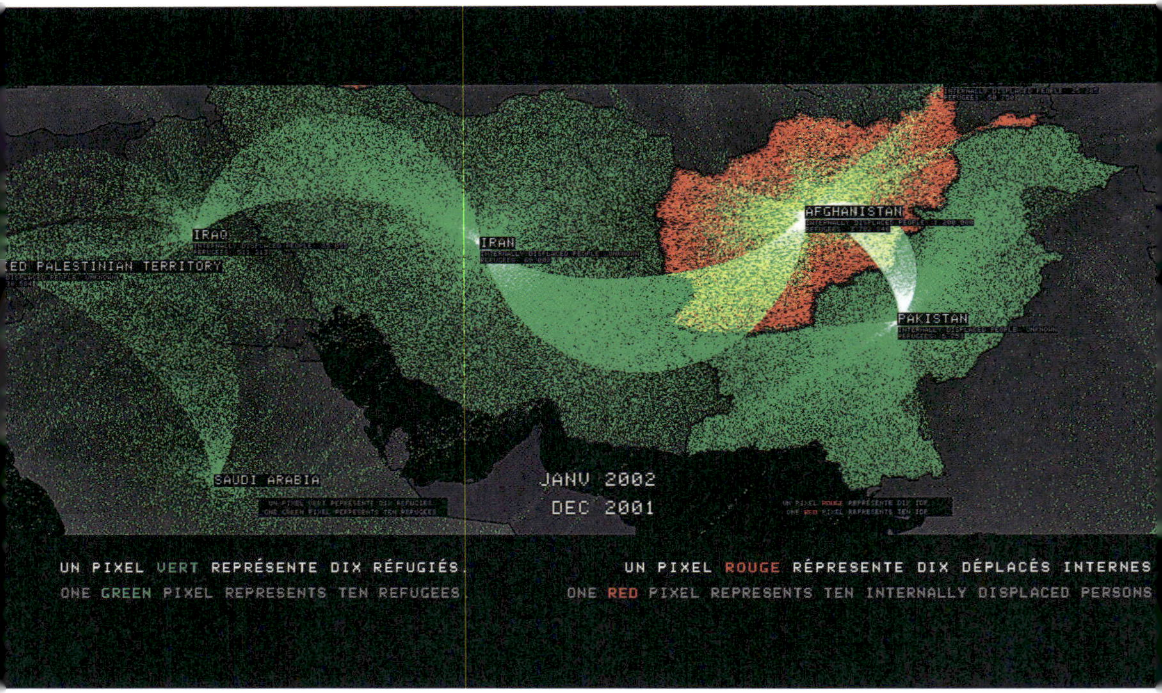
IRAQ
IRAN
AFGHANISTAN
PAKISTAN
ED PALESTINIAN TERRITORY
SAUDI ARABIA
JANV 2002
DEC 2001
UN PIXEL VERT REPRÉSENTE DIX RÉFUGIÉS.
ONE GREEN PIXEL REPRESENTS TEN REFUGEES.
UN PIXEL ROUGE RÉPRESENTE DIX DÉPLACÉS INTERNES
ONE RED PIXEL REPRESENTS TEN INTERNALLY DISPLACED PERSONS

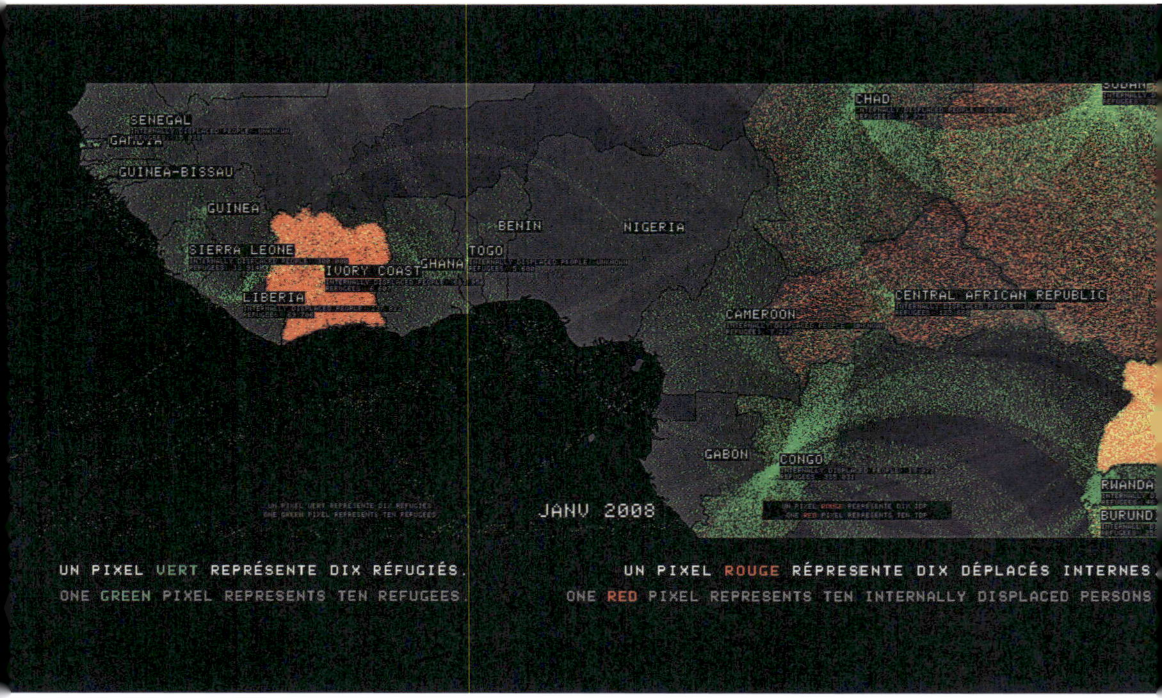
SENEGAL
GAMBIA
GUINEA-BISSAU
GUINEA
SIERRA LEONE
IVORY COAST
GHANA
LIBERIA
TOGO
BENIN
NIGERIA
CHAD
CENTRAL AFRICAN REPUBLIC
CAMEROON
GABON
CONGO
RWANDA
BURUND
JANV 2008
UN PIXEL VERT REPRÉSENTE DIX RÉFUGIÉS.
ONE GREEN PIXEL REPRESENTS TEN REFUGEES.
UN PIXEL ROUGE RÉPRESENTE DIX DÉPLACÉS INTERNES.
ONE RED PIXEL REPRESENTS TEN INTERNALLY DISPLACED PERSONS

Map *Political Refugees and Forced Migration* by Diller Scofidio + Renfro, Mark Hansen, Laura Kurgan, and Ben Rubin, in collaboration with Robert Gerard Pietrusko and Stewart Smith

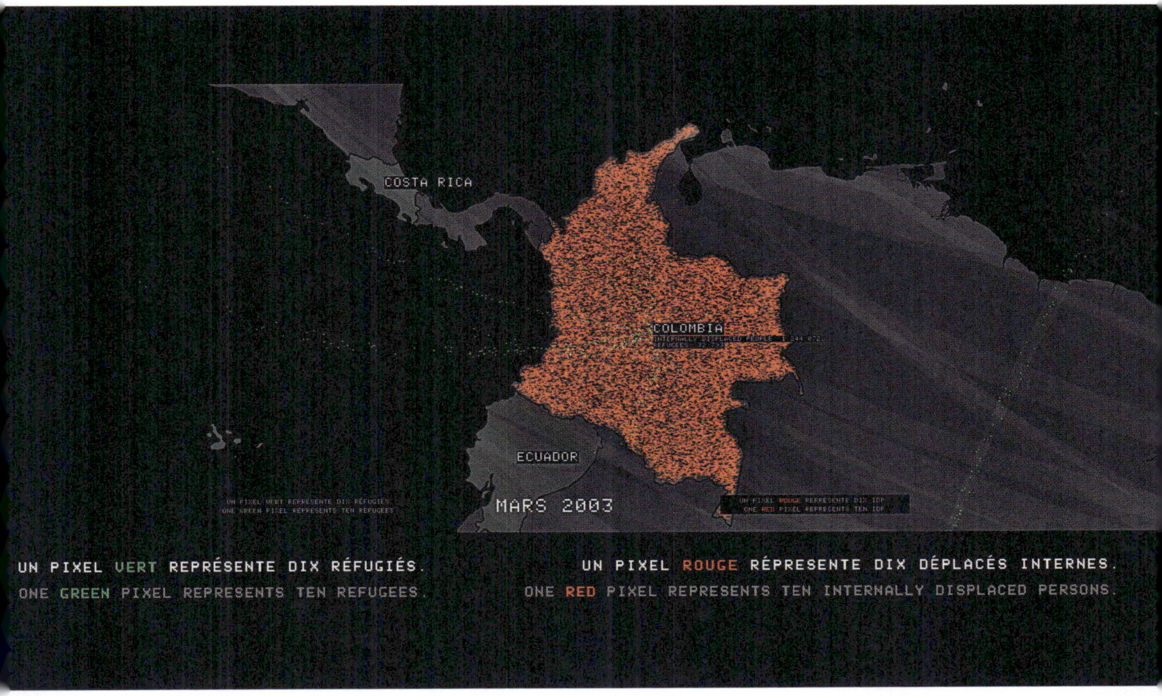

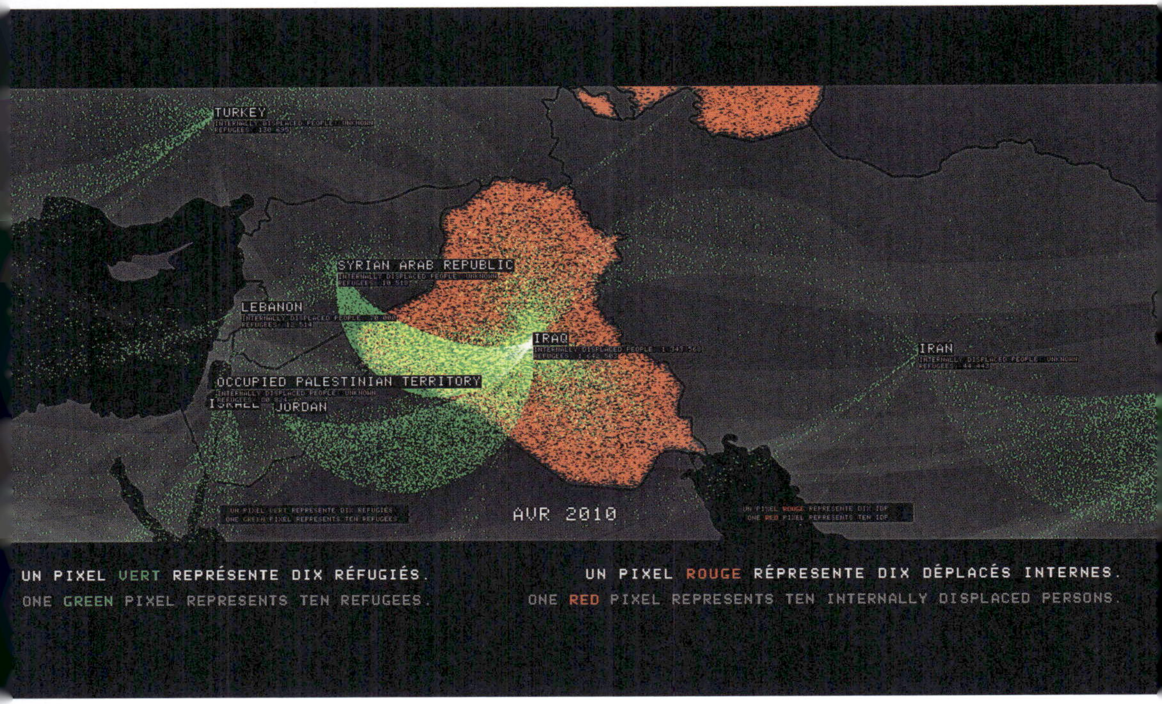

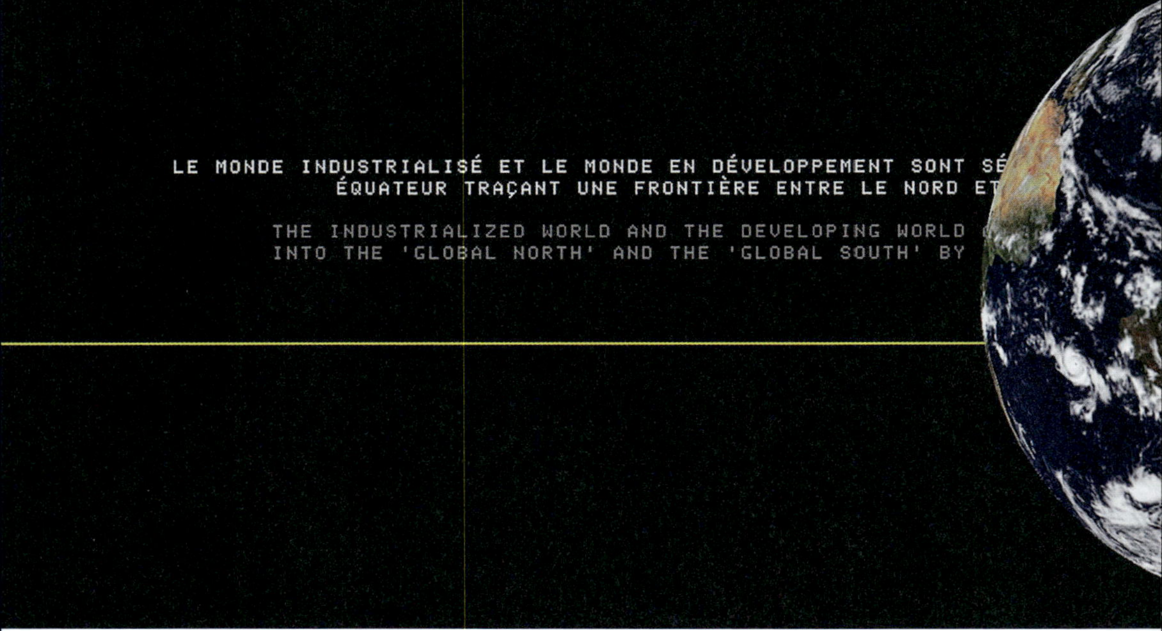

Natural Disasters

Since 2008, natural disasters displace on average 26 million people per year—or one person every second. This map shows that developing countries pay a disproportionate toll to natural disasters compared to industrialized countries. First, the animation shows the number of people around the world affected and displaced by storms, droughts, and earthquakes. The spinning globe then traces a line that divides the world into the developed "Global North" and developing "Global South."

Blue bubbles appear on the map representing flood events, which displaced 124 million people between 2006 and 2014. Floods in the Global South are compared to floods of the same magnitude in the Global North, revealing significant differences in the number of displaced people. For example, a magnitude 6.6 flood displaced 90 people

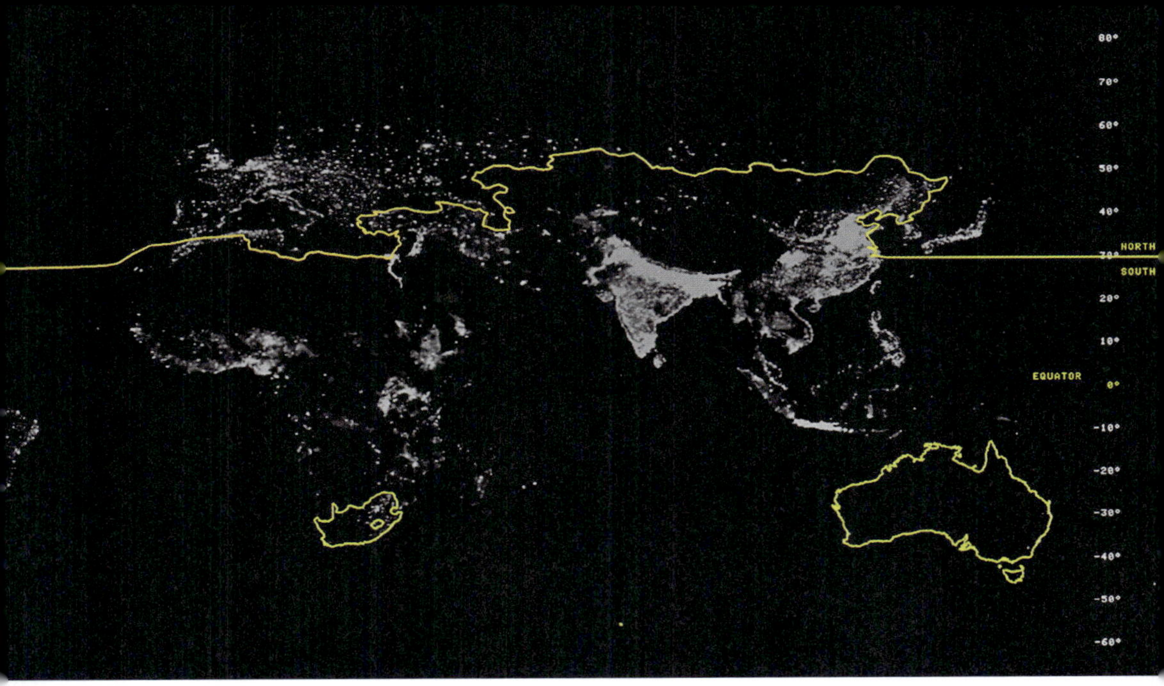

in Australia in 2007, while a flood of the same magnitude displaced 14 million people in Pakistan in 2010. In other words, the victims and damages are much more significant in the Global South than in the Global North—clearly a factor of poverty versus wealth and the absence of government infrastructure.

Data sources: EM-DAT, The Emergency Events Database: Centre for Research on Epidemiology of Disasters (CRED), Université Catholique de Louvain, École de Santé Publique / Dartmouth Flood Observatory, Active Archive of Large Floods / Project of Risk Evaluation, Vulnerability, Information and Early Warning (PREVIEW), Division of Early Warning and Assessment (DEWA), Global Resource Information Database (GRID) / Earthquakes Hazards Program by the US Geological Survey (USGS) / Historical Hurricane tracks data, National Weather Service by National Oceanic and Atmospheric Administration (NOAA)

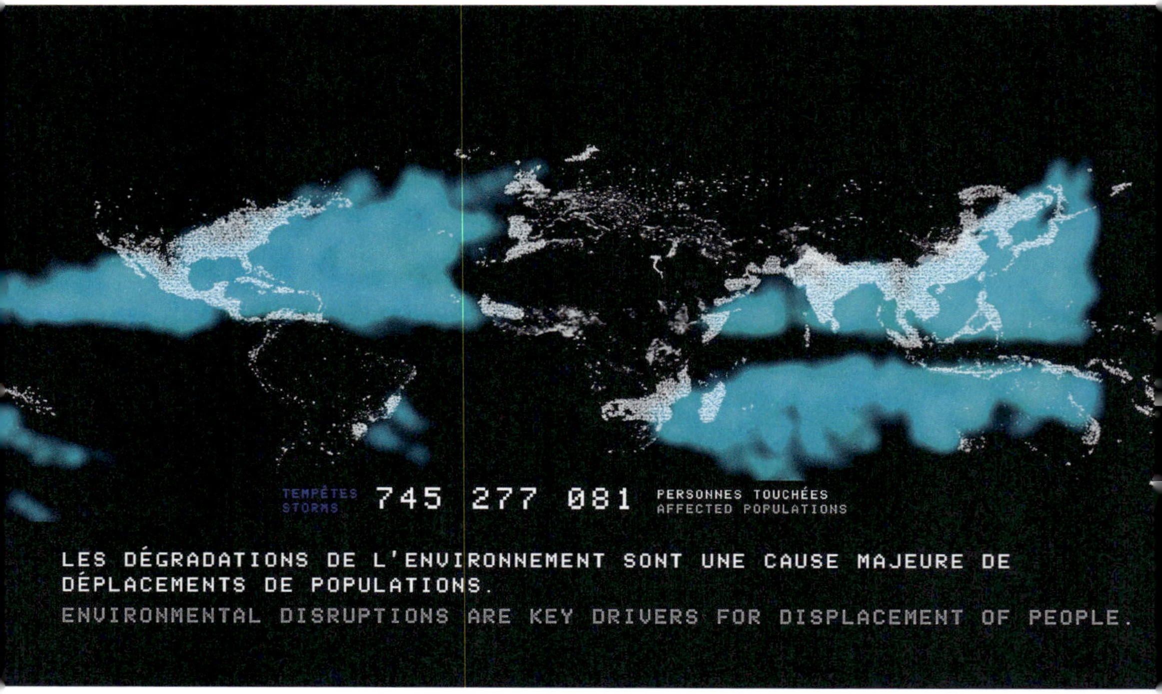
TEMPÊTES
STORMS
745 277 081
PERSONNES TOUCHÉES
AFFECTED POPULATIONS
LES DÉGRADATIONS DE L'ENVIRONNEMENT SONT UNE CAUSE MAJEURE DE DÉPLACEMENTS DE POPULATIONS.
ENVIRONMENTAL DISRUPTIONS ARE KEY DRIVERS FOR DISPLACEMENT OF PEOPLE.

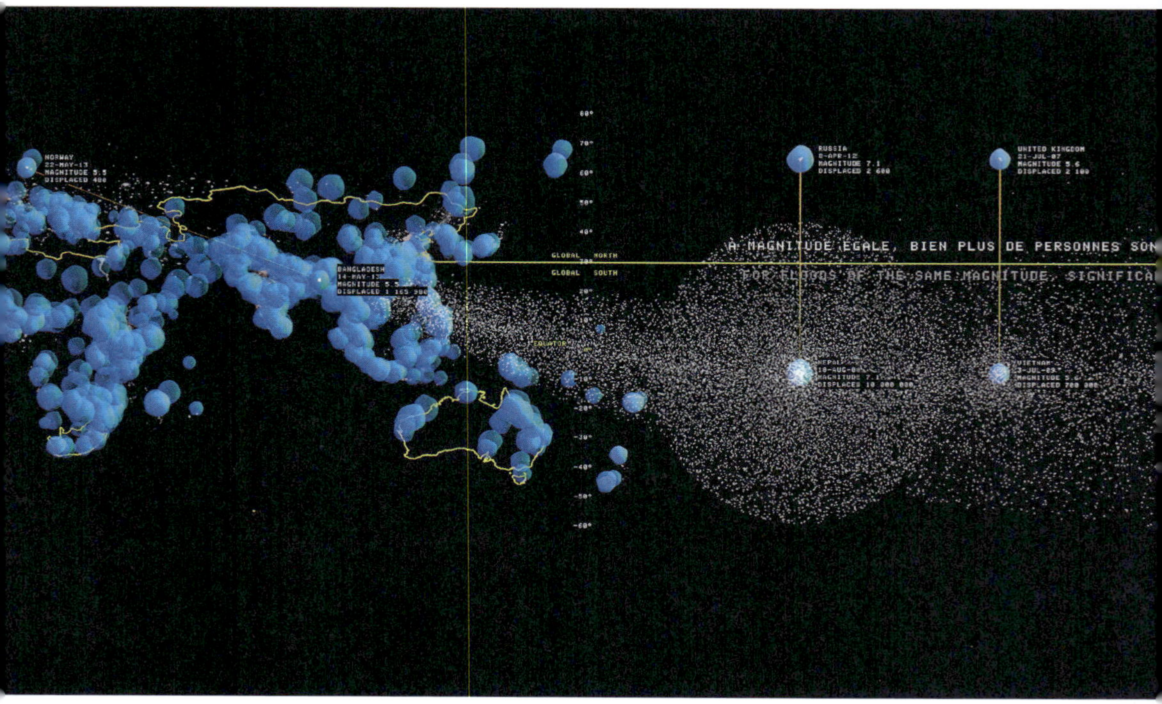
NORWAY
22-MAY-13
MAGNITUDE 5.5
DISPLACED 400
BANGLADESH
GLOBAL NORTH
GLOBAL SOUTH
EQUATOR
RUSSIA
8-APR-12
MAGNITUDE 7.1
DISPLACED 2 600
UNITED KINGDOM
21-JUL-07
MAGNITUDE 5.6
DISPLACED 2 100
A MAGNITUDE EGALE, BIEN PLUS DE PERSONNES SON
FOR FLOODS OF THE SAME MAGNITUDE, SIGNIFICA
DISPLACED 10 000 000

Map *Natural Disasters* by Diller Scofidio + Renfro, Mark Hansen, Laura Kurgan, and Ben Rubin, in collaboration with Robert Gerard Pietrusko and Stewart Smith

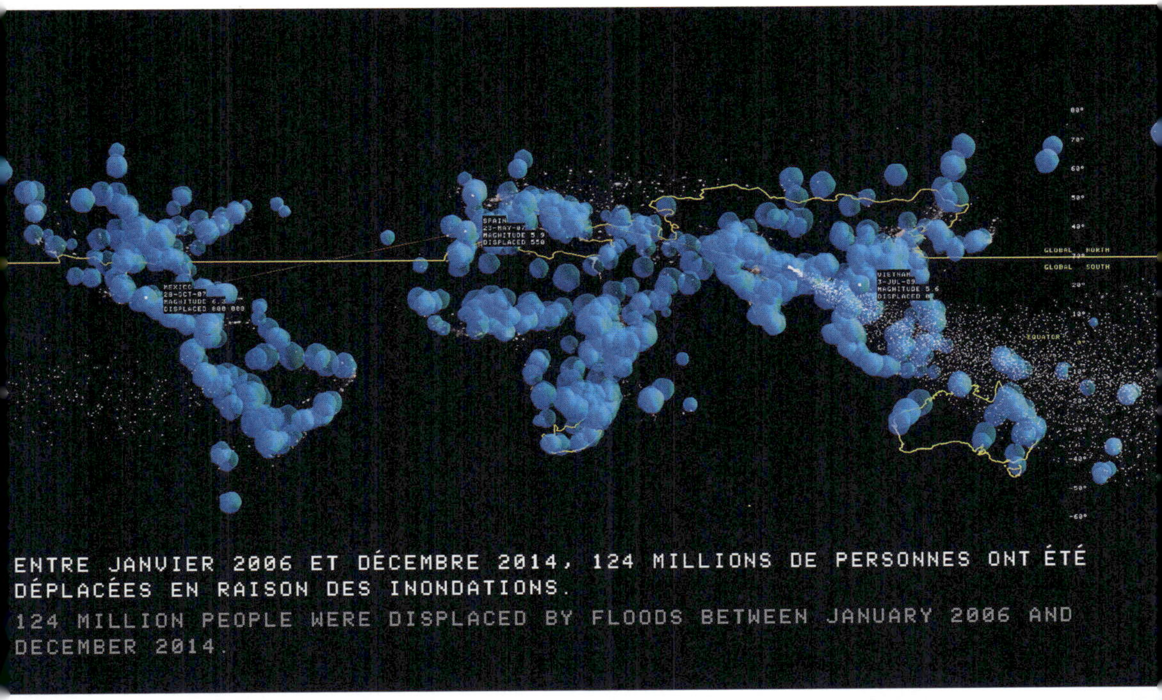

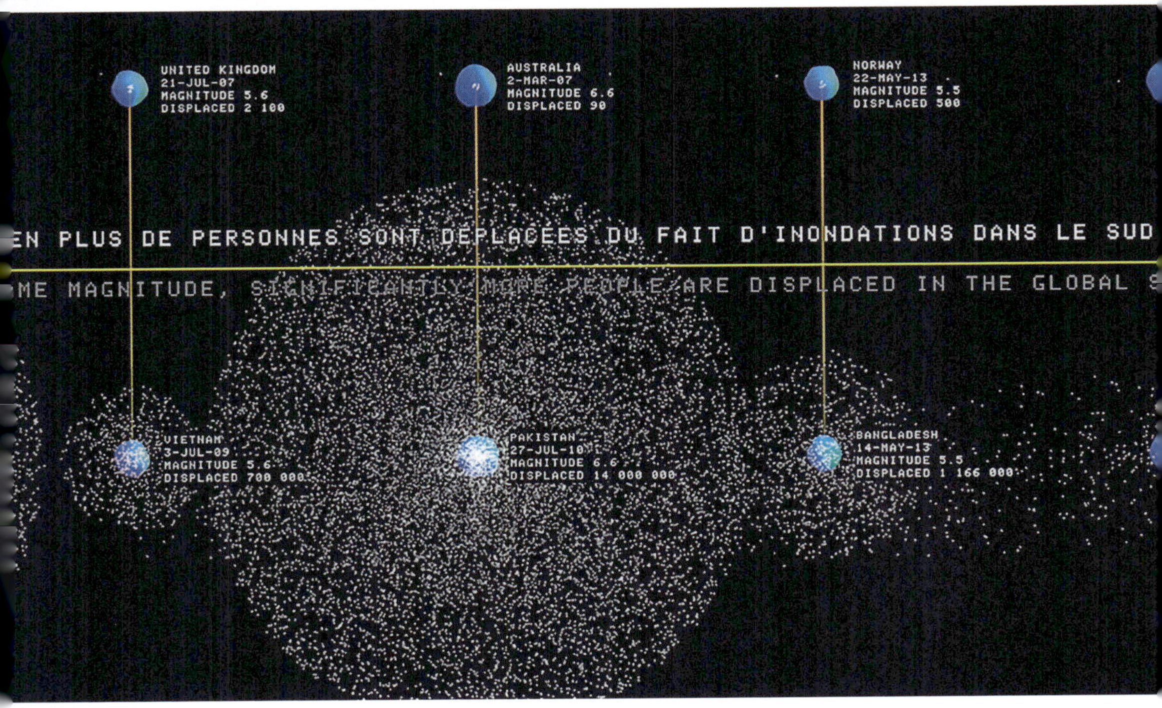

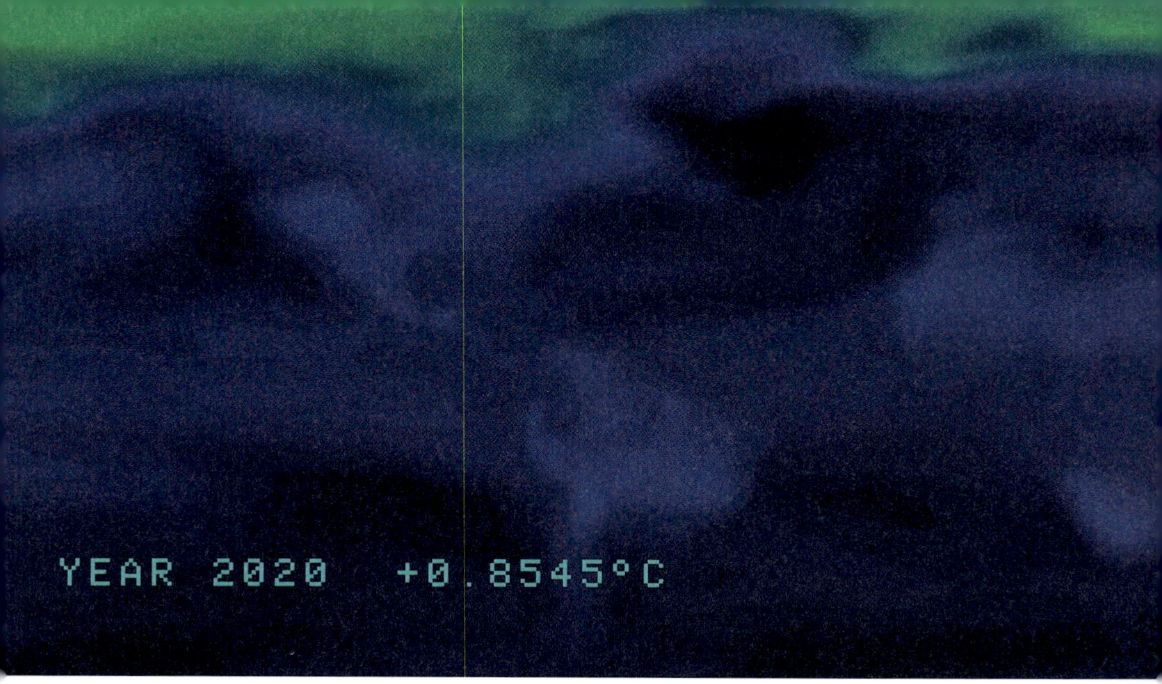

Rising Seas, Sinking Cities
Current rates of greenhouse gas emissions put the world on a course of predicted average warming of at least 3.5°C by 2100. As greenhouse gases warm the planet, the oceans are also warming up. The combined effects of the melting polar icecaps and the thermal expansion of water will cause sea levels to rise an estimated one meter by the end of the twenty-first century.

To explain the primary process contributing to the rise in sea levels, clouds of carbon emission expand around certain cities and countries and display their unequal contribution to the atmosphere. Next, thermal maps visualize the spatial patterns of rising temperatures. These maps are based on climate simulation models and present a sequence of predictions at five-year intervals between 2000 and 2100. Temperature rise is more pronounced in the North.

Given the premise that a one-centimeter rise in sea level could put a million people at risk of displacement, the subsequent scene displays the nearly ten thousand cities located within 100 kilometers of the coast. Collectively, these cities house one and a half billion people, or 25 percent of the global population. Which cities are most

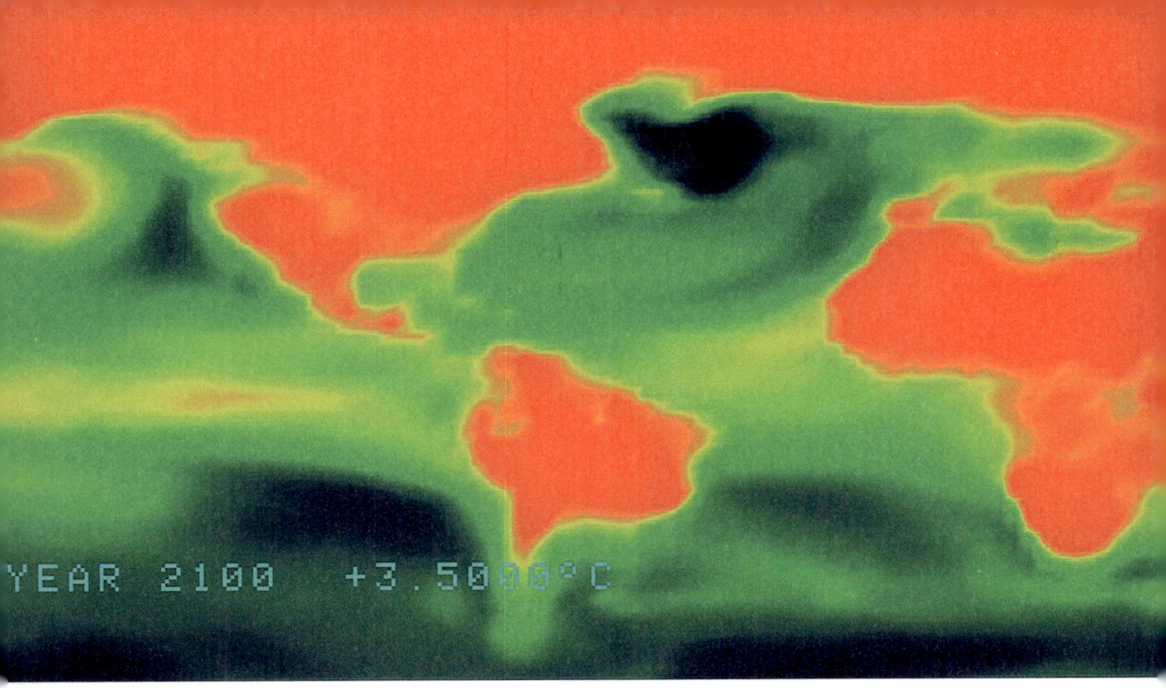

vulnerable? In order to answer this question, the cities are stretched to surround the room and displayed in elevation. One meter of water fills the room from the ground up, submerging the cities within that elevation zone. Some cities rise out of the water—those that may have a decreased risk relative to the ones clearly more vulnerable below.

Data sources: Global Rural-Urban Mapping Project, version 1 (GRUMP) – Settlement Points: Center for International Earth Science Information Network (CIESIN), Columbia University; International Food Policy Research Institute (IFPRI); The World Bank; Centro Internacional de Agricultura Tropical (CIAT), 2004 **/** Model for the Assessment of Greenhouse-gas Induced Climate Change, A Regional Climate SCENario GENerator **/** Geographically based Economic data (GEcon I.3) **/** Self-assessment matrix: Discovering a hotspot, Climate Resilient Cities, The World Bank, East Asia and Pacific Region **/** CO2 emissions: Carbon Dioxide Information Analysis Center, Oak Ridge National Laboratory (Gregg Marland, Tom Boden, and Bob Andres) **/** The Elevation Query Web Service, USGS Earth Resources Observation and Science (EROS) by the US Geological Survey (USGS) **/** Gridded Population of the World, version 3 (GPWv3) – National Boundaries, Center for International Earth Science Information Network (CIESIN), Columbia University; International Food Policy Research Institute (IPFRI); The World Bank; Centro Internacional de Agricultura Tropical (CIAT)

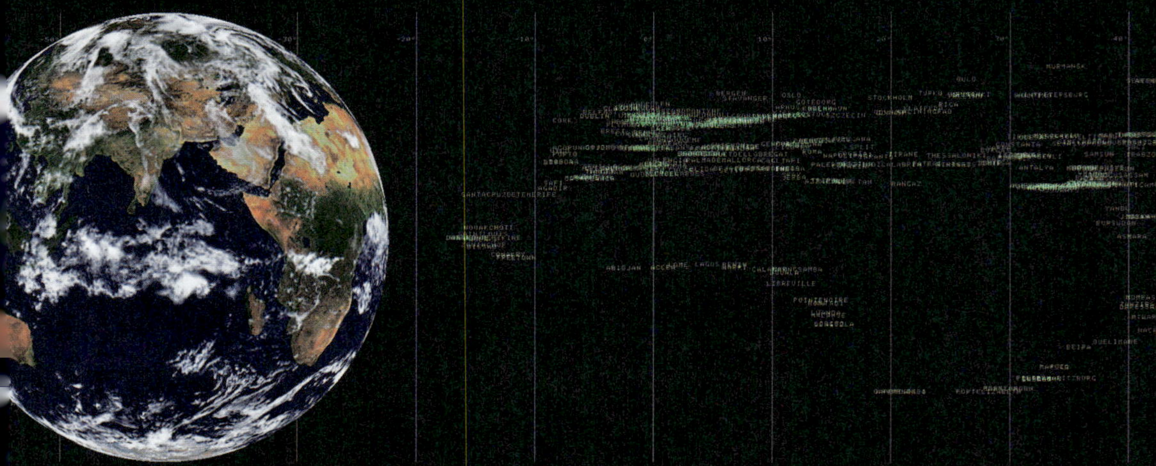

9000 VILLES SONT SITUÉES À MOINS DE 100 KM DE LA MER.

9000 CITIES ARE WITHIN 100 KM OF THE OCEAN.

D'ICI 2100, LA HAUSSE MOYENNE DU NIVEAU DE LA MER SERA DE 1 MÈTRE.

BY 2100, THE AVERAGE LEVEL OF THE SEA WILL HAVE RISEN BY 1 METER.

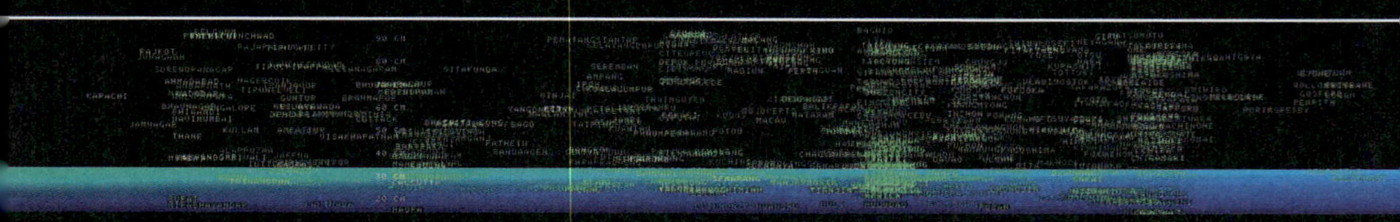

Map *Rising Seas, Sinking Cities* by Diller Scofidio + Renfro, Mark Hansen, Laura Kurgan, and Ben Rubin, in collaboration with Robert Gerard Pietrusko and Stewart Smith

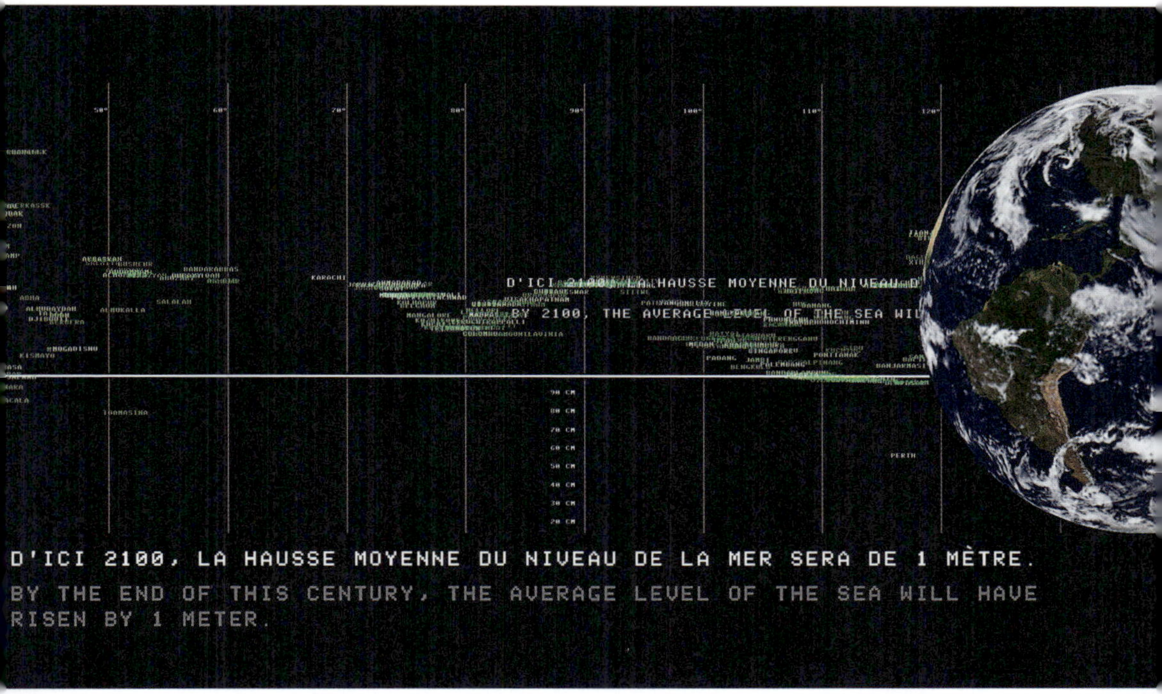

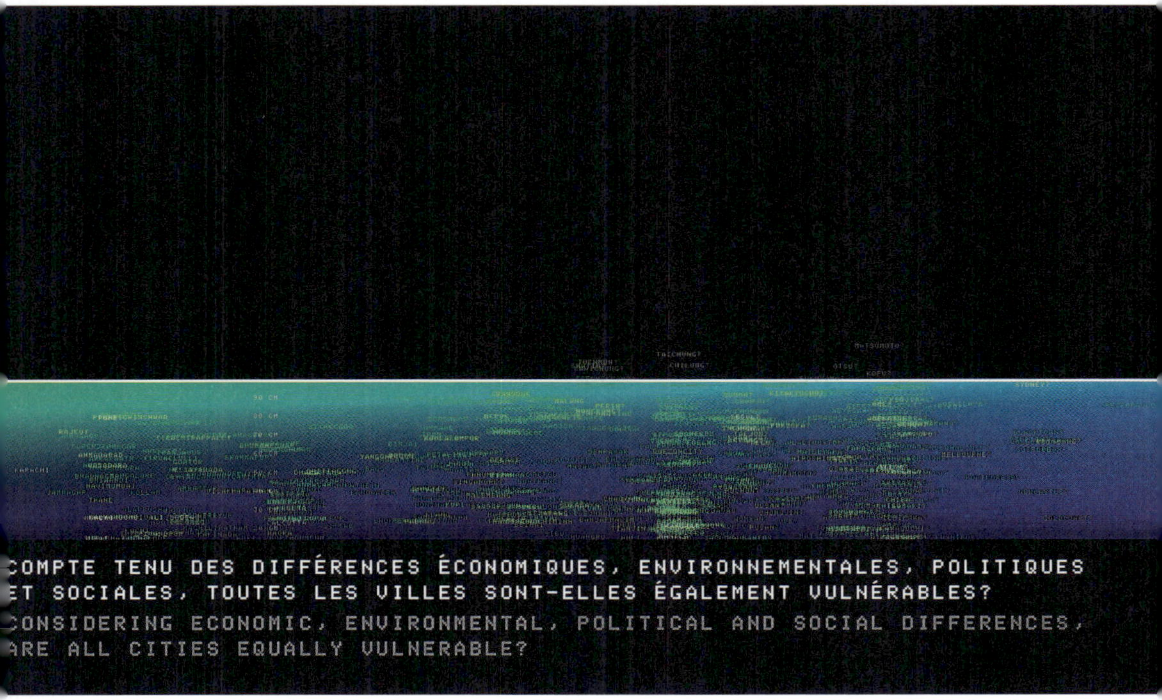

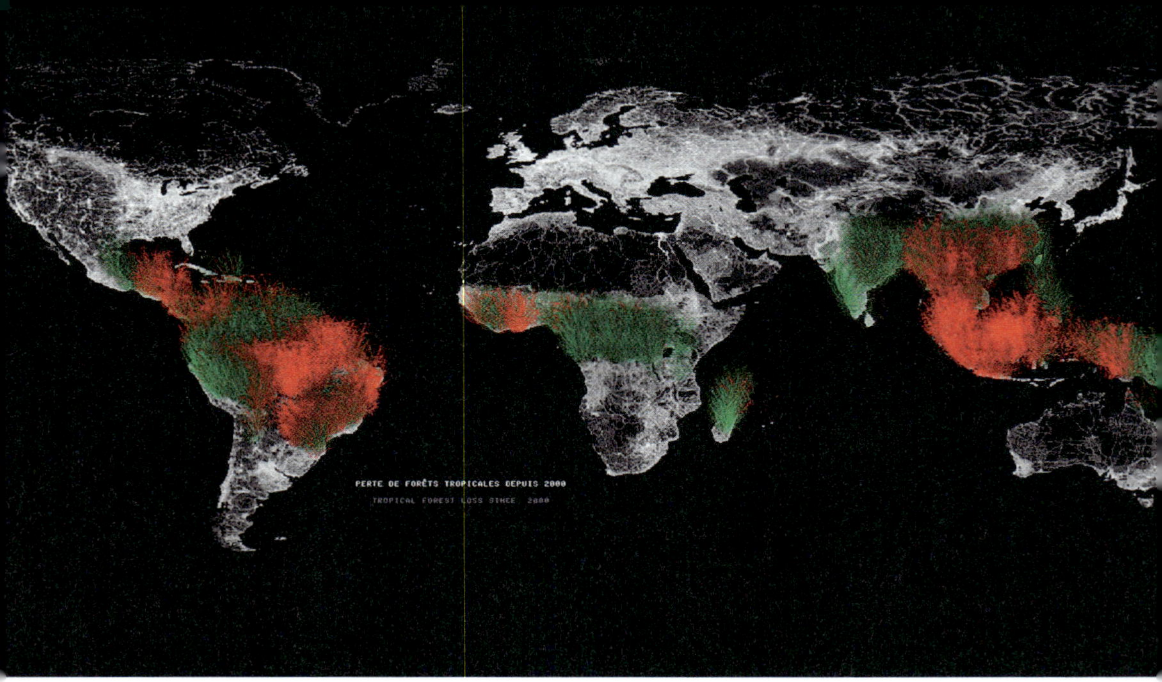

Speechless and Deforestation

Scientific Consultants: Bruce Albert (IRD) and François-Michel Le Tourneau (CNRS)

Tropical rainforests are concentrated across South America, Central Africa, and Southeast Asia. They are home to many indigenous people and contain 90 percent of the Earth's biodiversity. They are also vital for climate protection. Tropical deforestation alone creates one-fifth of global greenhouse gas emission. The ongoing decimation of these complex and fragile ecosystems, mainly due to agricultural development and logging, threatens many indigenous people's livelihoods, cultures, and languages. Tropical countries lose tree-cover every year—almost 10 million hectares in 2014, an area about the size of South Korea. Burning and logging are the primary vectors of destruction.

This map shows the ongoing process of tropical deforestation in three different regions: Xingu Park in Brazil, Southeast Cameroon, and Jambi Province in Sumatra, Indonesia. In each of these regions, indigenous peoples are at risk, as well as their cultures and languages. For example, fifty-six Xinguano villages in Brazil are threatened by the advance of soybean fields and pasture in 2013. Fifteen Amerindian languages spoken in Xingu Park are endangered. Trumai and Yawalapiti are under threat of extinction.

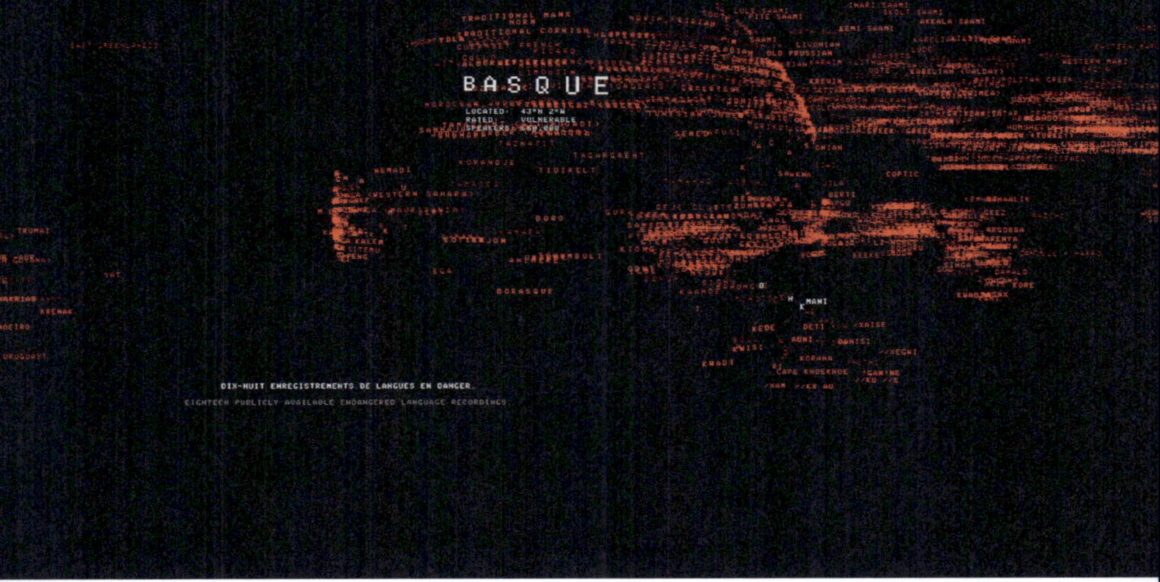

The last map shows that 96 percent of the world's 6,700 languages are spoken by 3 percent of its peoples, more than half of which are in danger of extinction by the end of the century. A list within this scene then displays 2,700 endangered languages, along with 230 that have gone extinct since 1950. A magnifying glass homes in on several endangered languages, triggering a recording of a person speaking in that tongue. Slowly the sound fades out and the map dissolves to black and the installation restarts from the beginning.

Data sources: UNESCO, *Atlas of the World's Languages in Danger*, 2009 / World Wildlife Fund (WWF) – Indonesia and Setiabudi (2015) Sumatra Forest and Land Cover Change 1985-2014 Database / Komunitas Konservasi Indonesia WARSI (KKI WARSI) / Forest Peoples Programme (FPP) / World Wildlife Fund (WWF) – Central Africa Office, Cameroon / Instituto Socioambiental (ISA) / Instituto Nacional de Pesquisas Espaciais (INPE), Projeto PRODES 2014 / Human Footprint and Last of the Wild v2: Wildlife Conservation Society (WCS), Center for International Network (CIESIN), Columbia University, 2002; International Food Policy Research Institute (IFPRI); The World Bank; Centro Internacional de Agricultura Tropical (CIAT) / NASA MODIS 32-day Composites, The Global Land Cover Facility: University of Maryland, College Park, Maryland / Global MODIS hotspot/fire location data: Fire Information for Resource Management System (FIRMS), University of Maryland

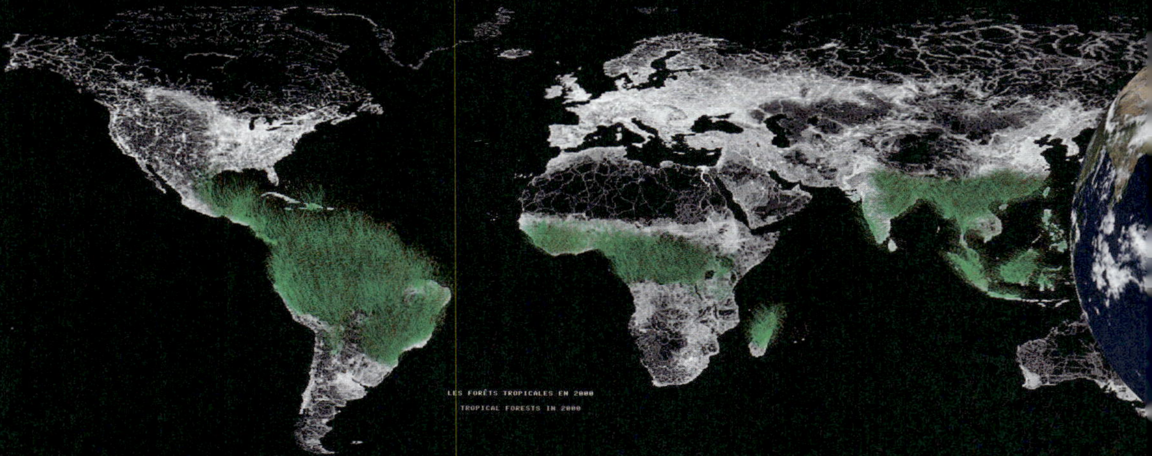

LES FORÊTS TROPICALES EN 2000

TROPICAL FORESTS IN 2000

LES FORÊTS TROPICALES SONT VITALES POUR LA PROTECTION DES PEUPLES INDIGÈNES, DE LA BIODIVERSITÉ ET DES CLIMATS.

TROPICAL FORESTS ARE VITAL FOR THE PROTECTION OF INDIGENOUS PEOPLES, BIODIVERSITY, AND THE CLIMATE.

U	MILTU	MOHAWK (WA_	MPI	NALU	NGANGIKURU_	NORFOLK-PI_	NU
	MINDIRI	MOJO	MRA	NALUO	NGARDI	NORMAN	NU
TZINCA	MINGRELIAN	MOK (CHINA)	MRU	NAMAN	NGARINMAN	NORN	NU
	MINHE MONG_	MOK (LAO P_	MT. IRAYA_	NAMBIQUARA_	NGARINYIN	INUPIAQ	NU
LE	MINYONG	MOK (MYANM_	MUDA	NAMBIQUARA_	NGARLA	NORTH ALAS_	NU
	MIQIE	MOKILESE	MUDBURRA	NAMONUITO	NGARLUMA	NORTH ALAS_	NU
	MIRAA (BR_	MOKLEN	MUINANE	NAMUYI	NGATIKESE_	NORTH FRIS_	NU
ANA (_	MIRAA (CO_	MOKSELA	MUJI	NANAY	NGBERE (C_	NORTH GREE_	NU
ANA (_	MIRIT TAP_	MOKSHA	MULAHA	NANTI	NGBERE (P_	NORTH SAAMI	NY

. EN SITUATION CRITIQUE. ETEINTE.

CRITICALLY ENDANGERED. EXTINCT.

	MIRIWOONG	MOLALA	MULAM	NAPORE	NGBINDA	NORTH SLAV_	NY
ALI	MISANTLA T_	MOLISE CRO_	MULAO	NAPU	NGILE	NORTHEASTE_	NY
	MISING	MOLO	MUNDARI	NARAU	NGOMBE	NORTHERN A_	NY
	MISKITO (H_	MOMUNA	MUNDURUK	NARIM	NGONG	NORTHERN A_	NY
UNA (_	MISKITO (N_	MON	MUNICHI	NARPA	NGUON	NORTHERN A_	NY
UNA (_	MIXTEC OF_	MONO	MUNJI	NASARIAN	NGWABA	NORTHERN C_	NY
LN M_	MIXTEC OF_	MONO (EAST_	MUNSEE (CA_	NASKAPI	NHEENGATU_	NORTHERN E_	NY
	MIXTEC OF_	MONO (WEST_	MUNSEE (UN_	NATANZI	NHEENGATU_	HAIDA	NY
	MIXTEC OF_	MONTANA SA_	MUOT	NATAORAN	NIHALI	NORTHERN K_	AN
GUARA_	MIXTEC OF_	MOOSE CREE	MURIK	NATCHEZ	NILA (NILA_	NORTHERN M_	OB
GUARA_	MIXTEC OF_	MOPN (BEL_	MURSI	NATSILINGM_	NILA (SERA_	NORTHERN P_	OB
GUARA_	MIXTEC OF_	MOPN (GUA_	MUSAN	NAUETI	NINAM (BRA_	NORTHERN P_	OC

Map *Speechless and Deforestation* by Diller Scofidio + Renfro, Mark Hansen, Laura Kurgan, and Ben Rubin, in collaboration with Robert Gerard Pietrusko and Stewart Smith

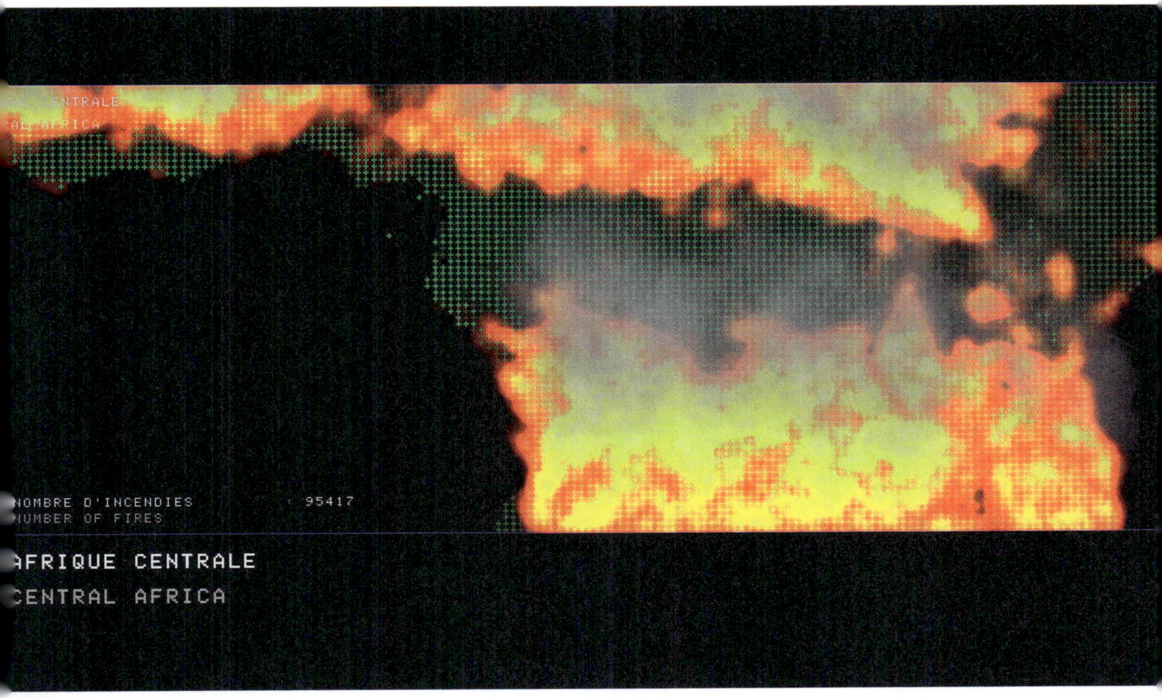

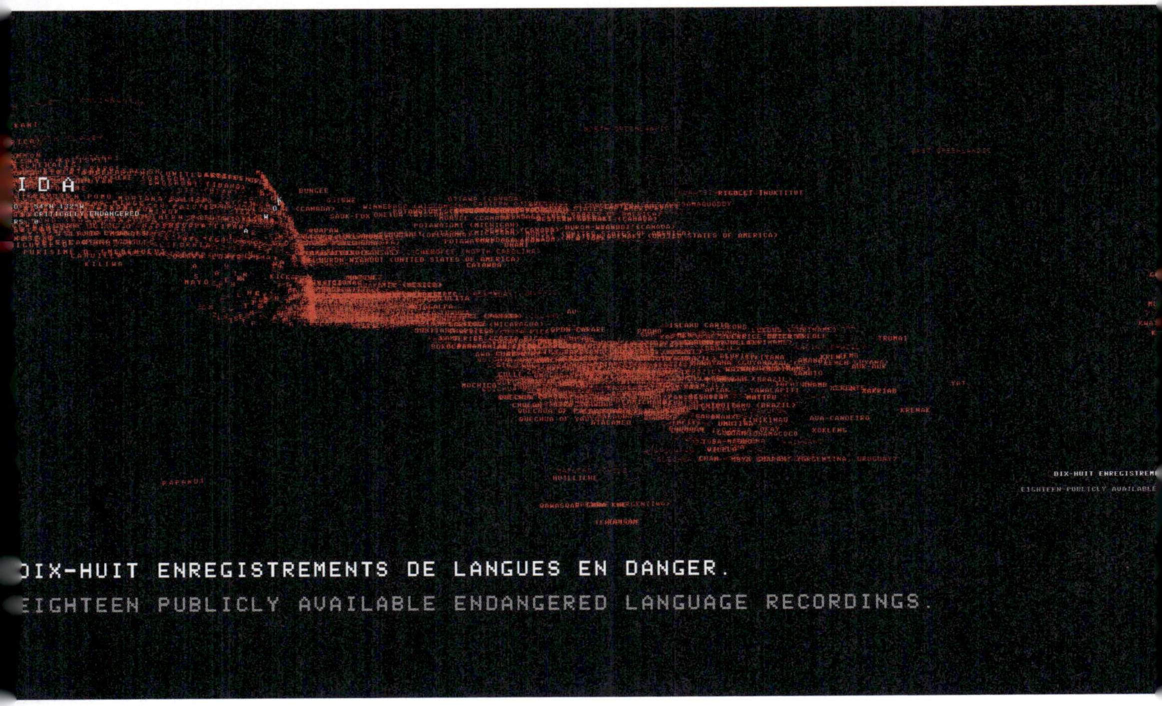

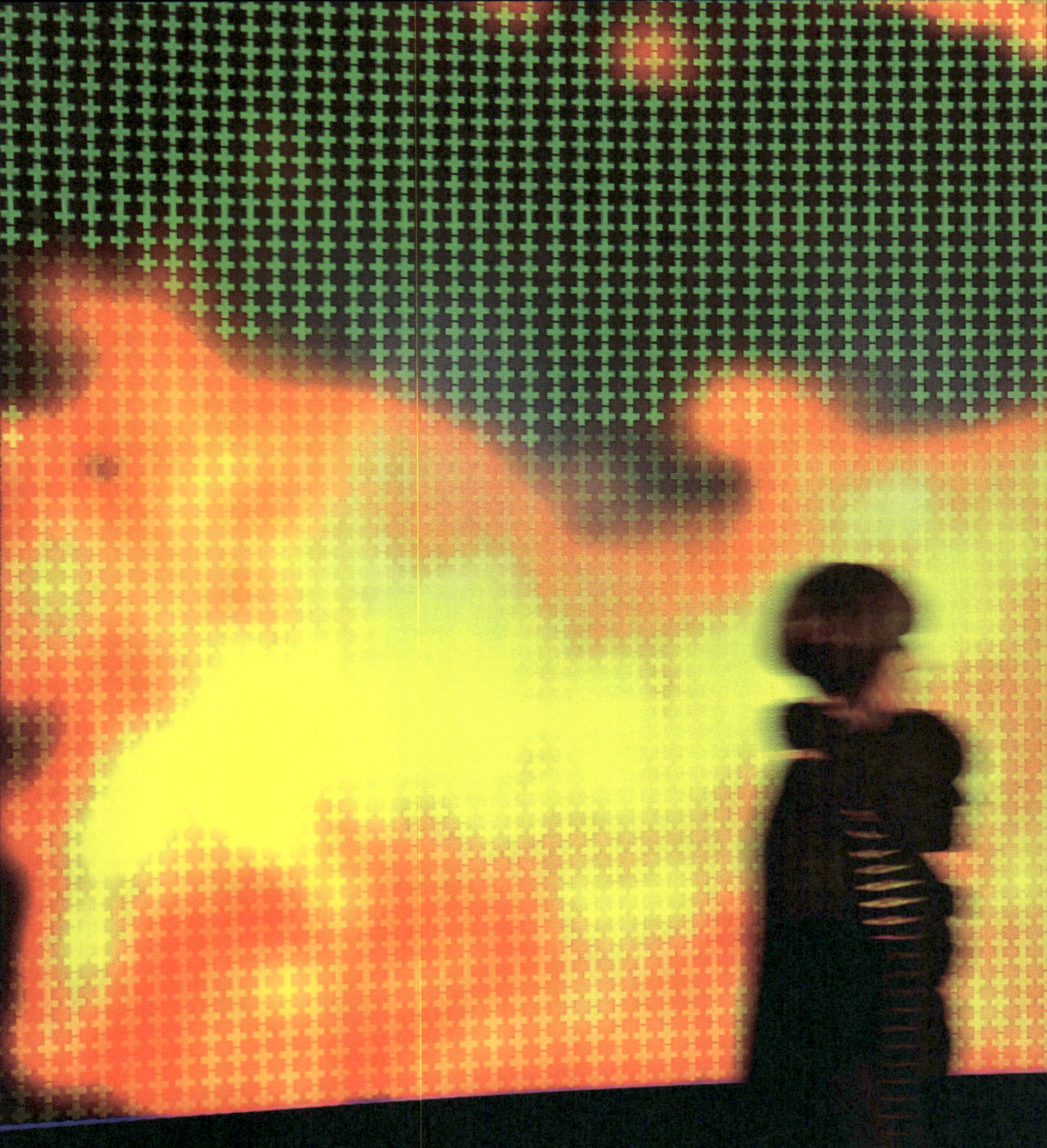

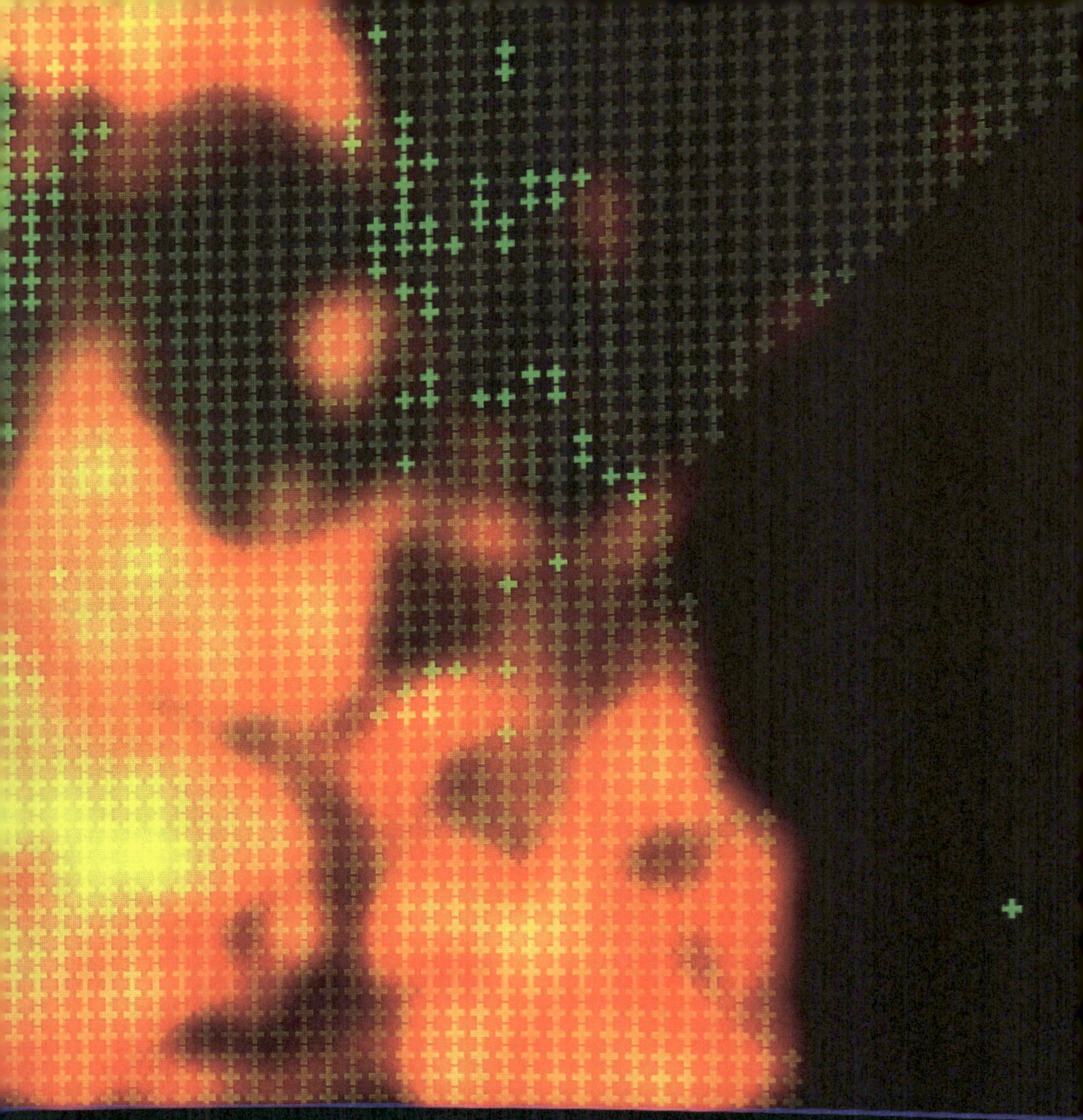

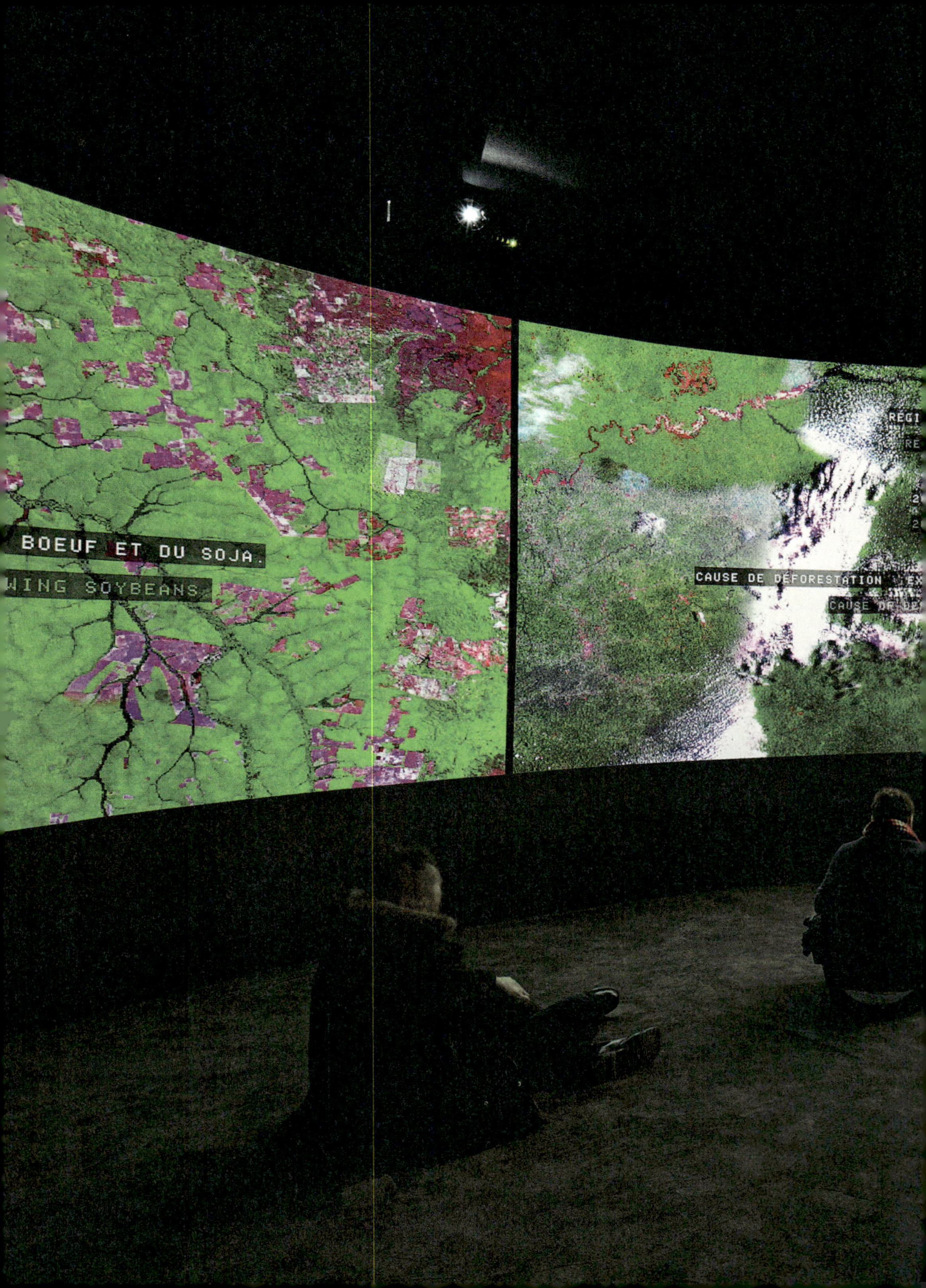
BOEUF ET DU SOJA.
WING SOYBEANS.
CAUSE DE DÉFORESTATION

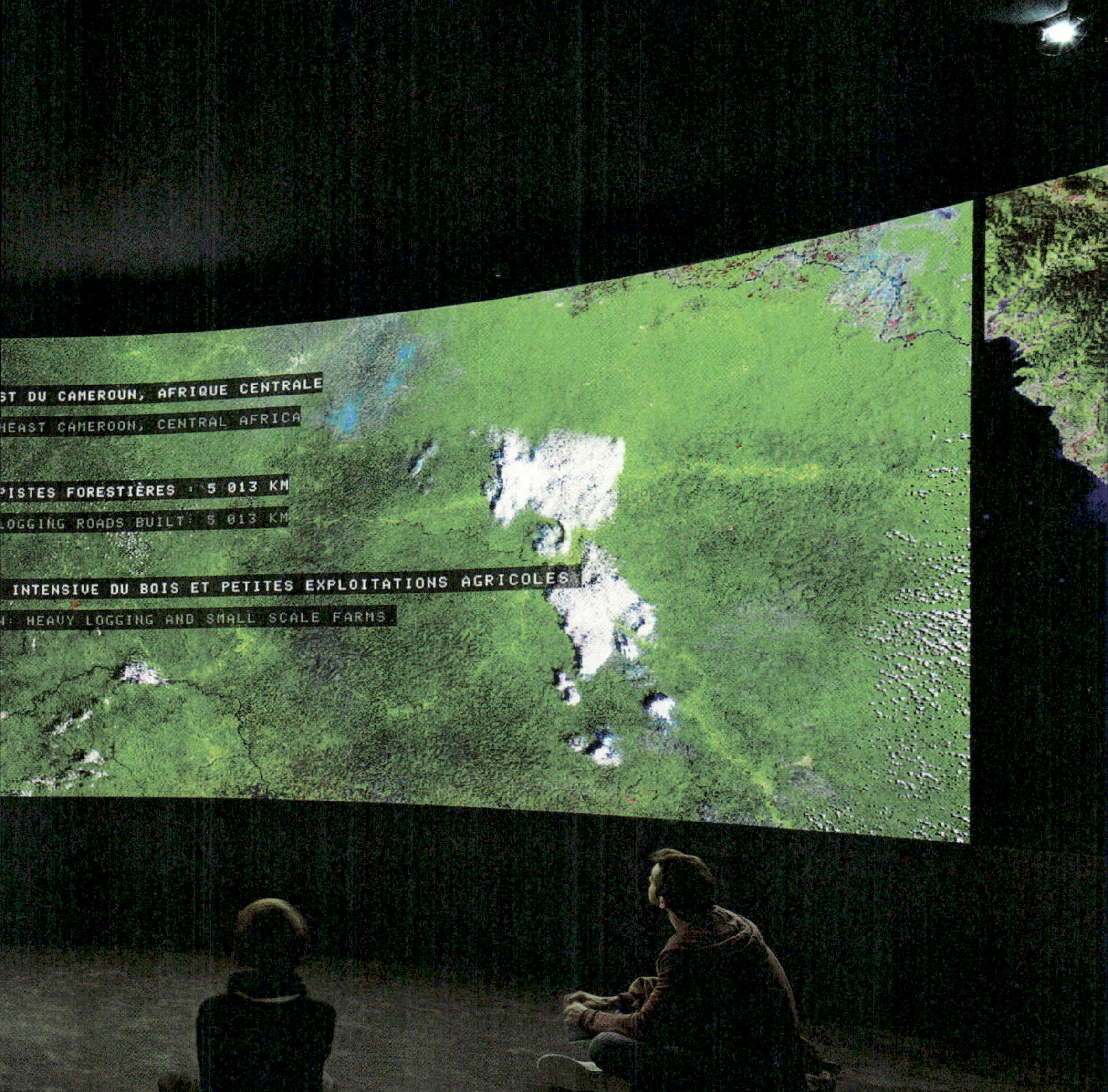
ST DU CAMEROUN, AFRIQUE CENTRALE
HEAST CAMEROON, CENTRAL AFRICA
PISTES FORESTIÈRES : 5 013 KM
LOGGING ROADS BUILT: 5 013 KM
INTENSIVE DU BOIS ET PETITES EXPLOITATIONS AGRICOLES
N: HEAVY LOGGING AND SMALL SCALE FARMS

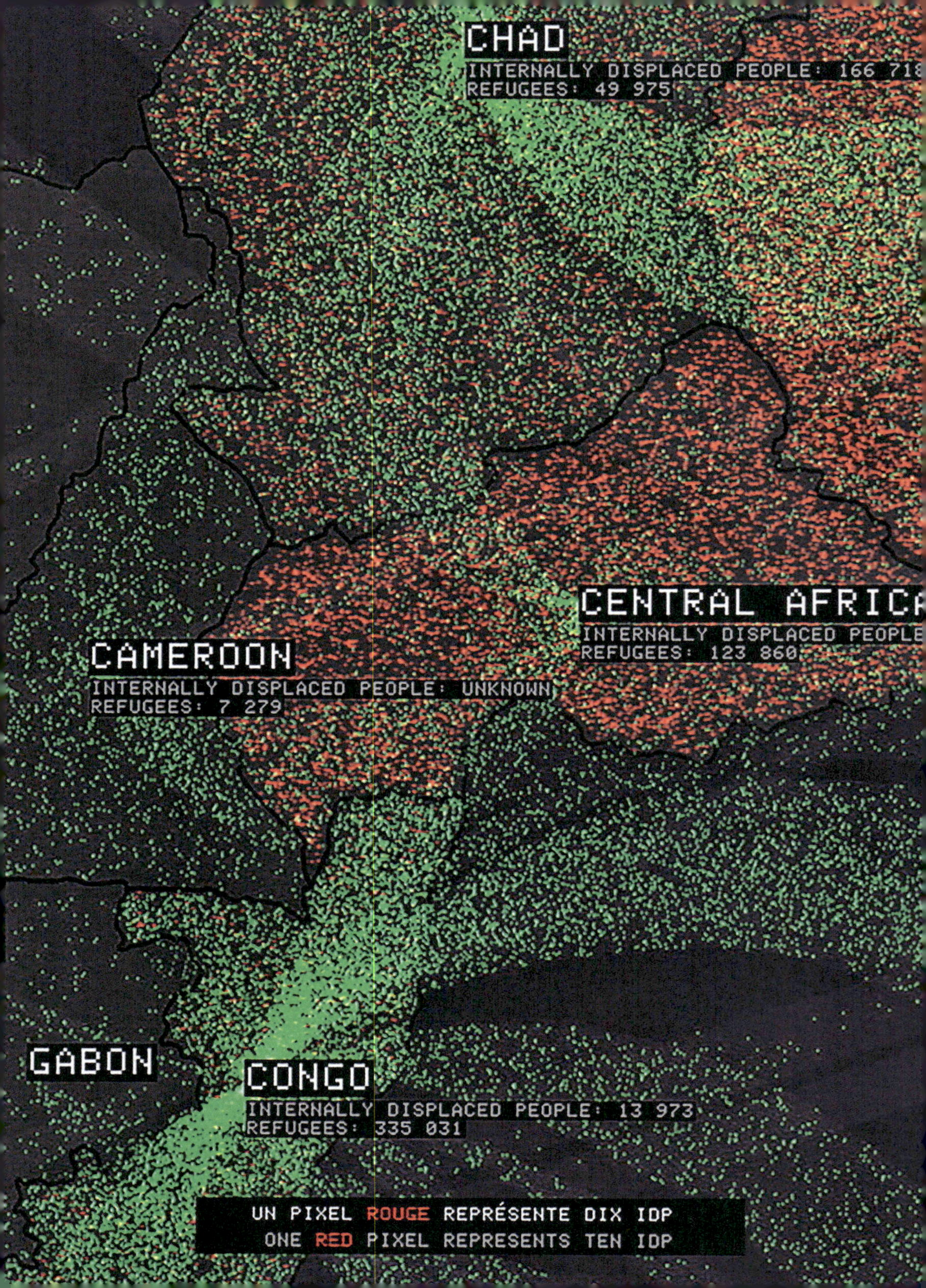
CHAD
INTERNALLY DISPLACED PEOPLE: 166 718
REFUGEES: 49 975
CENTRAL AFRICA
INTERNALLY DISPLACED PEOPLE
REFUGEES: 123 860
CAMEROON
INTERNALLY DISPLACED PEOPLE: UNKNOWN
REFUGEES: 7 279
GABON
CONGO
INTERNALLY DISPLACED PEOPLE: 13 973
REFUGEES: 335 031
UN PIXEL ROUGE REPRÉSENTE DIX IDP
ONE RED PIXEL REPRESENTS TEN IDP

Points of Reference

by François Gemenne

**Director of the Hugo Observatory at the University of Liège,
Co-director of the Observatory on Climate and Defence
of the French Ministry of the Armed Forces,
Lecturer at Sciences Po Paris and the Free University of Brussels,
Lead author for the IPCC 6th Assessment Report**

Walls

For an increasing number of governments, controlling and combating migration have become key priorities. Since the fall of the Berlin Wall, more than forty walls and barriers have been erected with a view to preventing migration. These walls and barriers are spread across the world: between the United States and Mexico, Botswana and Zimbabwe, China and North Korea, Saudi Arabia and Yemen, India and Bangladesh. They are also present in Europe: at the Hungarian border with Serbia, in the Spanish enclaves of Ceuta and Melilla, and around the entrance of the Channel Tunnel near Calais. These walls and barriers are hardly a rational response to unwanted migration, but they fulfill a symbolic function at a time when CCTV monitoring and human traceability are common. They have been proven inefficient and only make migration journeys more difficult and dangerous, but they have become the chimeric totems of an impregnable fortress: since the early 1990s, more than 40,000 migrants have perished on their way to Europe.

Migrants

Today, about 250 million people live outside of the country where they were born. This figure represents roughly 3 percent of the world's population. Migration is an extremely complex phenomenon, and migrants' journeys are increasingly fragmented through time and space. More people migrate every year—for very different reasons—but the rate of migrants in the world population has remained unchanged since the 1950s. It used to be much bigger before World War II: contrary to a common belief, migration is often reserved for the most privileged, and most international migrations are regional movements.

The causes of migration are very diverse: some leave to find a job, to pursue further education, or to look for a less hostile environment. Others leave to be reunited with their family, while some move for a limited period, in order to raise funds. Some migratory movements are cyclical, pendular, or seasonal. But millions of migrants do not choose to migrate: there are now more than 68 million forced migrants in the world, uprooted by wars, persecution, or natural disasters. A significant part of these forced migrants, however, do not cross a border, but are uprooted within their own country: they are internally displaced persons, or IDPs. There are an estimated 40 million IDPs worldwide; most of them are women and children. Unlike refugees, they do not benefit from any international protection, and are often the forgotten victims of a growing number of conflicts and natural disasters.

Undocumented

Since the mid-1970s, migration policies have been tightened up everywhere in the Western world. As new spaces were opened up for internal circulation, external borders were increasingly controlled in order to protect from a new type of so-called "invader": illegal migration. Most of those who cannot migrate in legal ways are unwilling to give up: desperate to save their life, recruited by smugglers, or hoping for a better future, thousands of migrants board rickety boats every year from Africa, to embark on a perilous journey to Europe. The desperate hope to reach the Spanish, Greek, or Italian coastline makes them risk their lives. Sometimes the journey ends dramatically, and the sea brings only corpses to the shores of Lampedusa, Turkey, or the Canary Islands. It is estimated that more than 40,000 migrants have perished in the Mediterranean Sea since the early 1990s—more than

3,500 in the year 2016. Some are luckier and are rescued by coast-guards, such as those clinging to a fishing net in the Mediterranean Sea, for example. Those who finally make it to their destination are often sent back to their country, or doomed to live in a clandestine way, hoping for a hypothetical regularization process. Europe is not the only place facing this phenomenon: the United States, but also countries such as Malaysia and Saudi Arabia experience similar situations. Most undocumented migrants have not crossed a border illegally, but have simply overstayed after the expiration of their visa. All share the hope of a better life.

Refugees

The number of forced migrants worldwide is constantly on the rise. Wars, violence, persecution, natural disasters, and poverty are amongst the factors that have driven millions away from their homes throughout the world. Not all, however, will be able to benefit from refugee status. The 1951 Geneva Convention, which is the principal instrument for refugee protection in international law, defines a refugee as someone fleeing one's country because of a well-founded fear of being persecuted for reasons of race, religion, nationality, membership in a particular social group, or political opinion. Those fleeing a natural disaster or staying within the borders of their own country, for example, cannot benefit from any specific protection. In 2018, there were an estimated 24.5 million refugees worldwide, including 6.3 million Syrians, 2.6 million Afghans, and 2.4 million South Sudanese. In addition to this number, there are 4.5 million Palestinian refugees still displaced in neighboring countries, as well as an estimated 40 million people displaced within their country, a number that is consistently rising. The combined number of refugees and internally displaced people is the highest ever recorded: more than 68 million people at the end of the year 2018.

Those displaced by environmental disruptions and natural disasters are not included in these figures: every year since 2008, 25 million people are displaced annually by natural disasters. That is one person every second, and this number does not account for people displaced by slow-onset environmental changes, such as sea-level rise or desertification. Whereas the number of forced migrants has reached an all-time peak, asylum regimes are experiencing a profound crisis: only a fraction of those seeking asylum in Europe receive refugee status, and the recent influx of refugees to the shores of Europe has induced a deep political crisis amongst European governments. Meanwhile, protracted refugee situations accumulate, as 86 percent of the world's refugees are hosted in developing countries.

Camps

Refugee camps are probably the most obvious symbols of the plight of refugees worldwide. Usually built in emergency situations by the United Nations High Commissioner for Refugees (UNHCR), governments, or humanitarian organizations and agencies, they provide a temporary shelter for populations displaced by conflicts or natural disasters. A single camp can sometimes be home to hundreds of thousands of people, and thus represents challenges for the security, hygiene, and alimentation of its residents. The refugee camp is, by nature, a temporary structure; protracted refugee situations are, however, increasingly common, and the camp then becomes a permanent habitat, a city in its own right, externalized. The average lifetime of a refugee camp is seventeen years. More than half of the world's refugees live in conditions of protracted displacement, often inextricable, without the possibility of returning home. Palestinian refugees, some of whom have been displaced for more than sixty years and whose refugee status is now hereditary, represent the most emblematic case of such situations. The camp is then the only horizon for those trapped in these forgotten situations.

Former UN High Commissioner for Refugees Gerrit van Heuven Goedhart once described these camps as "black spots" that should "burn holes in the consciences of all those privileged to live in better conditions."

Vulnerability

Amongst the numerous tragedies induced by Hurricane Katrina in 2005, here is one that has not been told: the disaster happened at the end of August, and not at the beginning of September. Paychecks had not been sent yet, and the poorest families lacked the financial resources to evacuate the city before it was flooded by the waters of Lake Pontchartrain. About 60,000 people who did not have the resources to leave, who did not have a car, or who just did not know where to go, ended up trapped in the water or packed in the city's football stadium in appalling conditions, before being scattered throughout the United States.

Though the hurricane affected the whole population of New Orleans, those most affected were the poor and people of color, the sick, and the elderly. Many of these people will never return to New Orleans. Across the world, the most vulnerable populations are those who will be first and most affected by climate change.

Vulnerability cannot be reduced to poverty: it is a set of conditions that create an unequal exposure to natural hazards for some populations. This is vulnerability that explains, for example, why an earthquake of a similar magnitude will result in more casualties in one country than in another: because there's no such thing as a "natural" disaster.

Melting of glaciers and ice caps

A polar bear floating on a block of ice has become one of the strongest symbols for climate change. Though the melting of the iceberg has no effect on sea-level rise—like an ice cube melting in a glass of water—it is a powerful reminder of one of climate change's most devastating effects: the melting of glaciers and ice caps. Since 2009, Antarctica has been losing more than 250 billion tons of ice every year—against "only" 40 billion in the 1980s. Today, the scenario of a complete melting of the Arctic and Antarctica can no longer be brushed off. Mountain glaciers are also badly affected, despite the key role they play in the provision of freshwater for many regions. Their melting will first induce an increase of river flow, but this will not last long: once the glaciers have melted, the regions around them can expect situations of water stress.

Climate change and sea-level rise

One of climate change's most obvious consequences is the rise of sea levels as the combined result of the oceans' thermic expansion and the melting of glaciers and ice caps. During the twentieth century, global sea levels have increased by 15–20 centimeters, and this increase will most likely rise above one meter by 2100. Even though estimates vary and the rise will not be uniform across the globe, partly because of fluctuations induced by the meteorological event El Niño, small island states are particularly at risk, and their very existence may be threatened. This is the

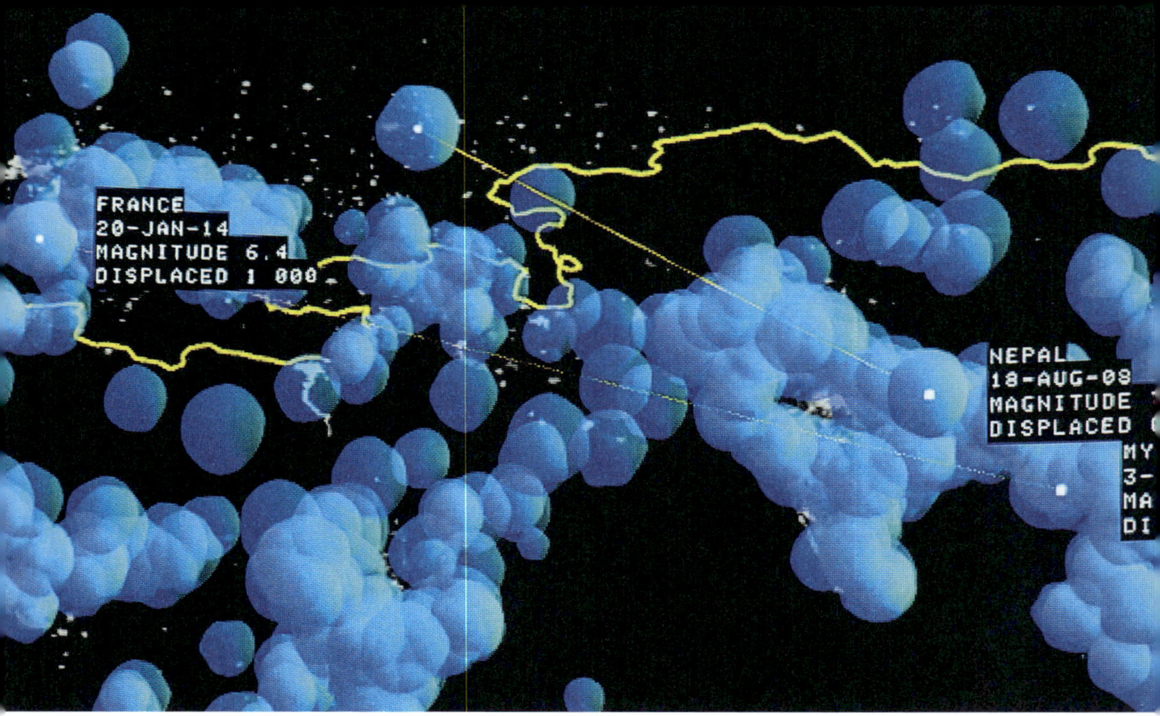

case for Tuvalu, a tiny archipelago in the middle of the South Pacific Ocean, and one of the world's smallest and flattest countries.

Tuvalu, whose greenhouse gas emissions are infinitesimal, also represents the fundamental injustice of climate change: industrialized countries bear most of the responsibility for global warming, yet developing countries, which bear only a negligible responsibility, will be the first victims of its impact.

It is now commonplace to blame emerging countries such as China, India, or Brazil. If we consider carbon emissions per capita however, rather than global emissions, another reality appears in which carbon emission inequalities persist: an American citizen's emissions are twice as high as a Chinese citizens', and the ratio between a Qatari citizen and an Indian citizen is as high as twenty-five to one. A fair climate regime, however, would entitle each inhabitant to the same emission levels, and thus to the same standards of living.

Desertification

Desertification is a forgotten environmental crisis, threatening about one third of the Earth's landmass. It is a complex phenomenon whose causes are both natural and human. Amongst these are climate variations, overgrazing, and inappropriate land use. The importance of the phenomenon will be considerably aggravated by climate change, which will induce a decrease in precipitations in many affected regions. Despite a UN Convention on the matter, desertification remains a forgotten problem, and measures to combat it have produced limited results.

The consequences of desertification are particularly dramatic in Sub-Saharan Africa. Every year, thousands of farmers and herders are forced to abandon their land and push into the major cities of the African continent. Some, supported by their families and sometimes an entire community, will attempt a perilous journey to migrate to Europe or the Persian Gulf countries. Most of them will have no other choice than to stay in their country, powerless to fight the progress of the desert.

Deforestation

Rainforests are the ecosystem in which the most animal and vegetal species live. It is also one of the ecosystems most at risk: every year, about 13 million hectares of forest are logged, mostly in Brazil, Indonesia, and the Congo. This massive deforestation threatens the world's biological diversity, but also the survival of indigenous peoples whose natural habitat is in the forest.

Without a doubt, it is in Amazonia that the situation is most critical. Since 1970, at least 600,000 square kilometers of rainforest have been lost. This deforestation, which spans an area larger than France, is due to several factors: logging, of course, but also cattle ranching, soybean production, and infrastructure projects, such as roads and dams. The effects are devastating: one third of the known animal and vegetal species live in the Amazonian rainforest, and many are now facing extinction. The livelihoods of indigenous people are also at risk: isolated Indians are kicked out of their homelands, and their way of life, their language—and sometimes their existence—are threatened.

Deforestation is also responsible for up to one fifth of the carbon dioxide concentration in the atmosphere. A logged tree no longer performs photosynthesis, the natural process of transformation of carbon into oxygen; instead it releases large quantities of carbon accumulated throughout its life into the atmosphere. It is estimated that deforestation in Amazonia is responsible for one tenth of global warming. This issue is of utmost importance in the fight against climate change.

Indigenous peoples

Because of their great dependence on their environment, indigenous peoples are among the first affected by climate change. While they are also the best observers of the phenomenon, they are too often neglected by climate policies. Their knowledge of the environment is an invaluable resource for the development of adaptation strategies on a global scale—provided that their voices are heard. There are more than six thousand languages registered worldwide, but half of them are facing extinction. Every week, a language becomes extinct. This impoverishment of linguistic diversity is directly related to the loss of biodiversity worldwide, and the threats to the environment. The subsistence of indigenous peoples is directly dependent on the ecosystems in which they live. Today, these ecosystems are threatened by deforestation in Amazonia, land tenure speculation in Argentina, desertification in Sub-Saharan Africa, and rising sea levels in the small island states. Consequently, the way of life of many people is at risk, including that of the Ayoreo in Paraguay, the Jarawa in the Andaman Islands, and the Enawene Nawe in Brazil.

Natural disasters

It is often said that natural disasters occur when a natural risk meets a social vulnerability. Is an earthquake in the middle of the desert a natural disaster? Or the flooding of uninhabited zones? For a natural disaster to occur, it has to affect vulnerable people.

Over the last decade, the number of natural disasters has been on the rise, while the number of environmental hazards remained relatively stable. In 2018, the EM-DAT database recorded 281 natural disasters in the world, affecting 60 million people across the world. These figures are expected to increase because of climate change, though the number of victims remains quite stable over time. Asia is by far the most affected continent. Natural disasters come in many shapes: floods, earthquakes, cyclones, droughts, and so on. They are the most brutal and devastating environmental disruptions, and one of the key drivers of population displacements across the world.

Text first published in the exhibition catalog
Native Land, Stop Eject (Paris: Fondation Cartier
pour l'art contemporain, 2008) and updated in 2019

François Gemenne jointly heads the Observatory on Climate and Defence of the French Ministry of the Armed Forces at IRIS. A specialist of environmental geopolitics and migration dynamics, he is also a FNRS senior research associate at the University of Liège, where he is the Director of the Hugo Observatory. He also lectures on environmental and migration policies in various universities, including Sciences Po (Paris and Grenoble) and the Free University of Brussels, where he holds the Bernheim Chair on Peace and Citizenship. He is also the director of the Sustainable Development series at Presses de Sciences Po.

As a lead author for the IPCC, his research deals mostly with environmental and migration governance. He has worked with populations displaced by environmental changes, including natural disasters, and the policies of adaptation to climate change.

He was the scientific advisor of the exhibition *Native Land, Stop Eject* at the Fondation Cartier pour l'art contemporain in Paris in 2008. He has consulted for several organizations, including the International Organisation of Migration (IOM), the Asian Development Bank (ADB), the World Bank, the ACP Observatory on Migration, and the British government (Foresight). In 2010, he was awarded the ISDT-Wernaers Prize for achievement in the communication of science to the general public.

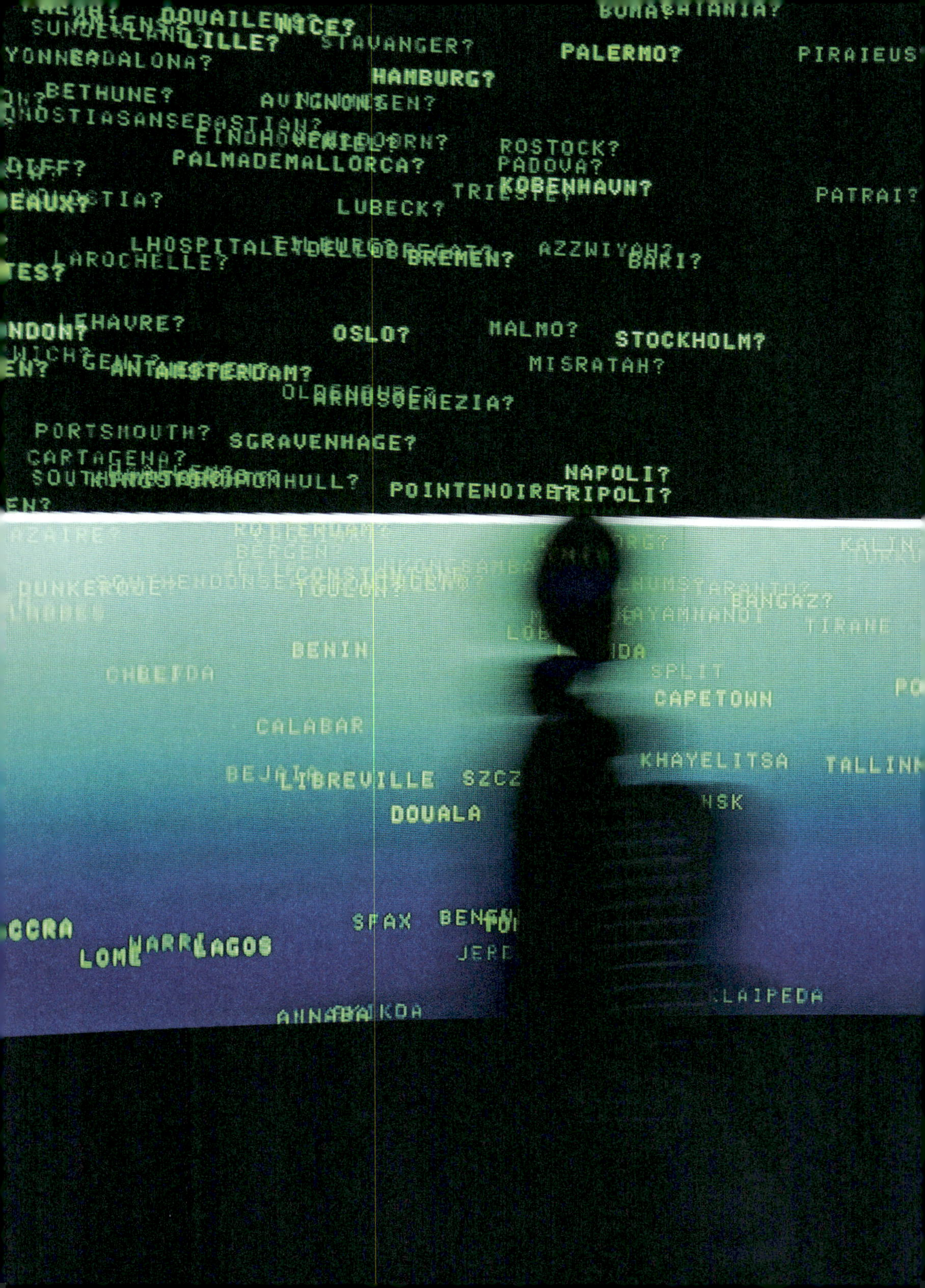
PALERMO?
PIRAIEUS
HAMBURG?
BETHUNE?
ROSTOCK?
PADOVA?
PALMADEMALLORCA?
KOBENHAVN?
PATRAI?
LUBECK?
BREMEN?
BARI?
LAROCHELLE?
LEHAVRE?
OSLO?
MALMO?
STOCKHOLM?
MISRATAH?
PORTSMOUTH?
SGRAVENHAGE?
CARTAGENA?
NAPOLI?
TRIPOLI?
BENIN
SPLIT
CAPETOWN
CALABAR
KHAYELITSA
TALLINN
LIBREVILLE
DOUALA
SFAX
LOME
LAGOS
KLAIPEDA

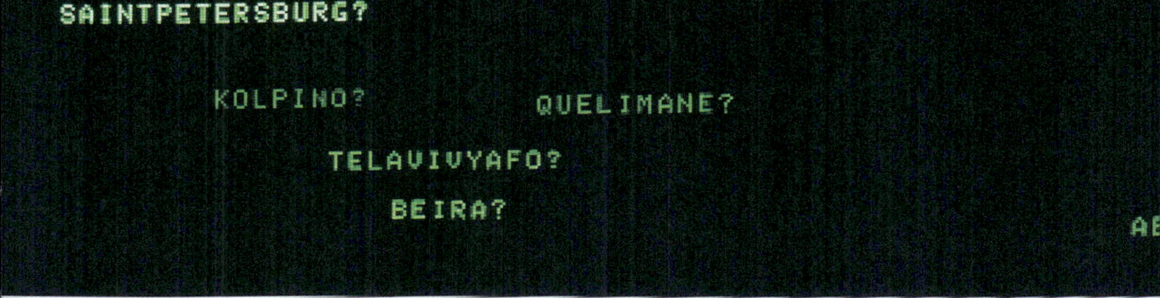
SAINTPETERSBURG?
KOLPINO?
QUELIMANE?
TELAVIVYAFO?
BEIRA?
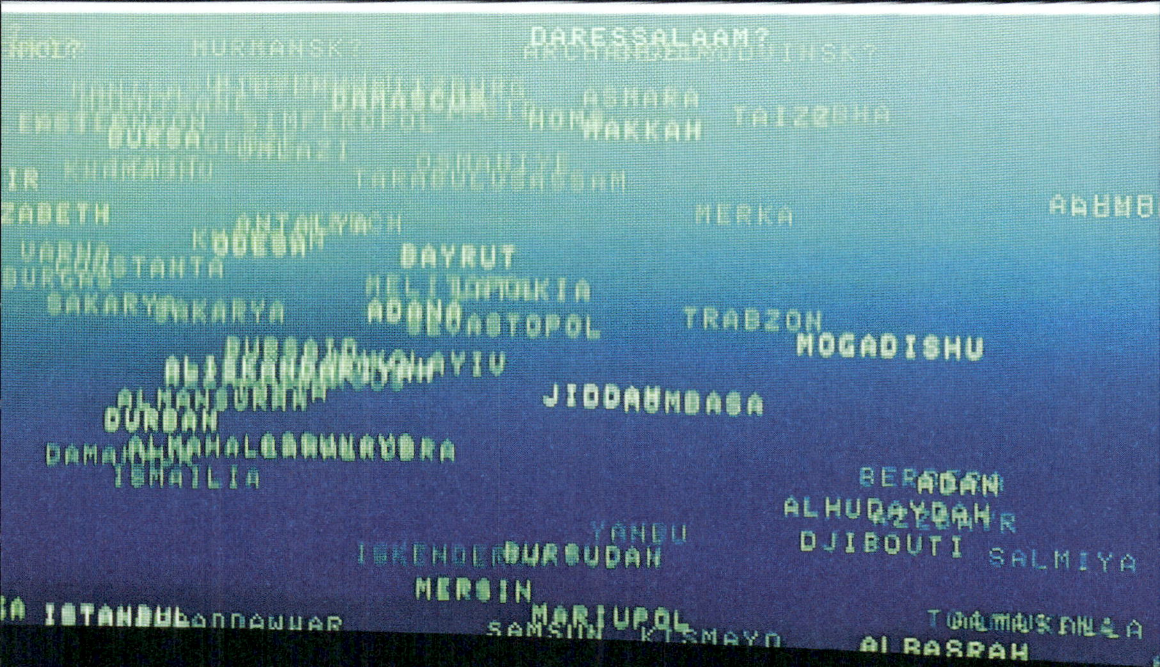
DARESSALAAM?
MURMANSK?
ASMARA
MAKKAH
MERKA
BAYRUT
TRABZON
MOGADISHU
SAKARYA
DURBAN
ISMAILIA
ADAN
ALHUDAYDAH
DJIBOUTI
SALMIYA
YANBU
MERSIN
MARIUPOL
ALBASRAH

"It's almost as though the sky, and the clouds in it and the pollution of it, were making their entry into history. Not the history of the seasons, summer, fall, winter, but of population flows, of zones now uninhabitable for reasons that aren't just to do with desertification, but with disappearance, with submersion of land. This is the future."

As Paul Virilio said, *EXIT* is a picture of a planet in trouble. The work addresses issues that have continued to intensify since its creation. It was updated entirely in 2015, reflecting the alarming evolution of the data since its first presentation in 2008. In each of the six maps, the connection between humans and their environment degraded considerably during these years. The number of people displaced by wars, persecutions, or natural disasters has reached an all-time peak since the end of World War II, leading to a major political crisis in Europe —although most of those displaced are hosted in developing countries. Urbanization and large-scale deforestation in tropical countries have continued at an accelerated pace, leading to the uprooting of an increasing number of indigenous communities and the resulting loss

Epilogue

of their native languages. It is estimated that more than half of the 6,700 languages still spoken today are in danger of extinction by the end of the twenty-first century.

EXIT also makes clear that climatic disruption, economic development, and movements of people, particularly from rural areas to urban zones, are interconnected. Natural disasters are displacing an average 26 million people per year, which equates to one person every second. *EXIT* highlights the growing importance of cities as populations grow. For the first time in history, more people now live in cities than in rural areas. Cities are key battlegrounds in the fight against climate change, as they now account for about 70 percent of global greenhouse gas emissions. Current political pledges to cut these emissions seem widely insufficient to achieve the goal of a maximum temperature increase of 2°C by the end of the twenty-first century, and scenarios of a global warming that could reach 4°C or even 6°C are no longer considered science fiction. A manifesto and a reality check of world disorders, *EXIT* is above all a call to preserve our native land.

KHAKAS
KHALING
KHAM
KHAMBA
KHAMNIGAN..
KHANG QUAN..
KHASALI
KHINALUG

KIOWA APAC..
KLALLAM
KLAMATH-MO..
KO
KOASATI (L..
KOASATI (T..
KOCH
KODAGU
KOFEI

KOSRAEAN
KOTA
KOTT
KOWAKI
KOYUKON
KRAOL
KRAVET
KRENAK
KRENJ
KREVIN
KRI
KRISTANG
KRONGO
KRUENG

KUNIGAMI
KUNJEN
KURRAMA
KURRIPAKO..
KURRU
KURTJAR
KURUYA
KURUBA
KUSUNDA
KUTENAI

LAGHU
LAGHUU
LAHA (LAO..
LAHA (SON..
LAI
LAIYOLO
LAJI
LAJIA
LAKE MIWOK
LAKHA
LAKOTA
LAMONGSE
LAMU

LI-NGBEE
LIGURIAN
LIKI
LIKUM
LILIALI
LILLOOET
LIMBU
LIMIRONG T..
LIMONESE C..
LIMOUSIN
LIPAN
LISELA
LISHAN DID..

LUA
LUDE
LUISE
LULE
LUMUN
LURI
LURO
LUSHO
MABIR
MACAG
MACHI
MACHI
MACUN

BLE. EN DANGER. SÉRIEUSEM

BLE. DEFINITELY ENDANGERED. SEVERELY

KHOJKI
KHOWA
KHVSGL U..
KHUNSARI
KHVARSHI
KHWE
KICKAPOO (..
KICKAPOO (..
KICKAPOO (..
KICKAPOO (..
KIJA
KIKSHT
KILDIN SAA..
KILEN
KILI
KILIT
KILIWA
KIM
KINARE
KINGS RIVE..
KINIKINAU
KINNAURI
KIONG
KIOWA

KOKE
KOKO BERA
KOKOTA
KOLAMI
KOLHRENG
KOM
KOMI
KOMO
KONA
KONDA
KONKOW
KONOMIHU
KORAGA
KORANA
KORANDJE
KORE
KOREGUAJE
KORO
KORONI
KOROSHI
KORYAK

KRYZ
//KU //E
KUA
KUAY
KUDU-CAMO
KUJARGE
KUJUBIM
KUK
KUKU YALAN..
KULFA
KULINA PNO
KULUI
KULUN
KUN LE
KUMZARI
KUNA (COLO..
KUNBARLANG
KUNDAL SHA..
KUNG

KUUKU YAU
KUURINJI
KUVI
KWADI
KWAKWALA
KWATAY
KWAZ
KWEGU
KWERISA
KWISI
KWADZA
//KXAU
KYAKALA
KEMANT
KICHE (M..
LAAL
LACANDN
LACHI
LADIN
LAE
LAEMAE
LAFOFA

LANGA
LANGTHANG..
LANGUEDOCI..
LANOH
LAOMIAN (C..
LAOMIAN (M..
LARDIL
LARI
LARO
LAUA
LAVUA
LAZ
LECO
LEMERIG
LENCA
LENGILU
LENGUA
LEPCHA
LHOKPU

LISHAN DID..
LISHANA DE..
LISHANA DE..
LISHANID N..
LISHANID N..
LISHPA
LIVONIAN
LOGOL
LOGORIK
LOGUDORESE
LOHORUNG
LOKE TIBET..
LOKONO
LOKONO (SU..
LOLAK
LOM
LOMBARD
LOREDIAKAR..
LORKOTI
LORRAIN
LOUN
LOWER CHEH..
LOWLAND CH..

MADNG
MAFEA
MAGAR
MAH M
MAHAS
MANIG
MAHON
MAIDU
MAJER
MAJHI
MAK
MAKAH
MAK
MAKO
MAKOL
MAKUR
MAKUA
MALAK
MALEC
MALEN
MALIN
MALIS

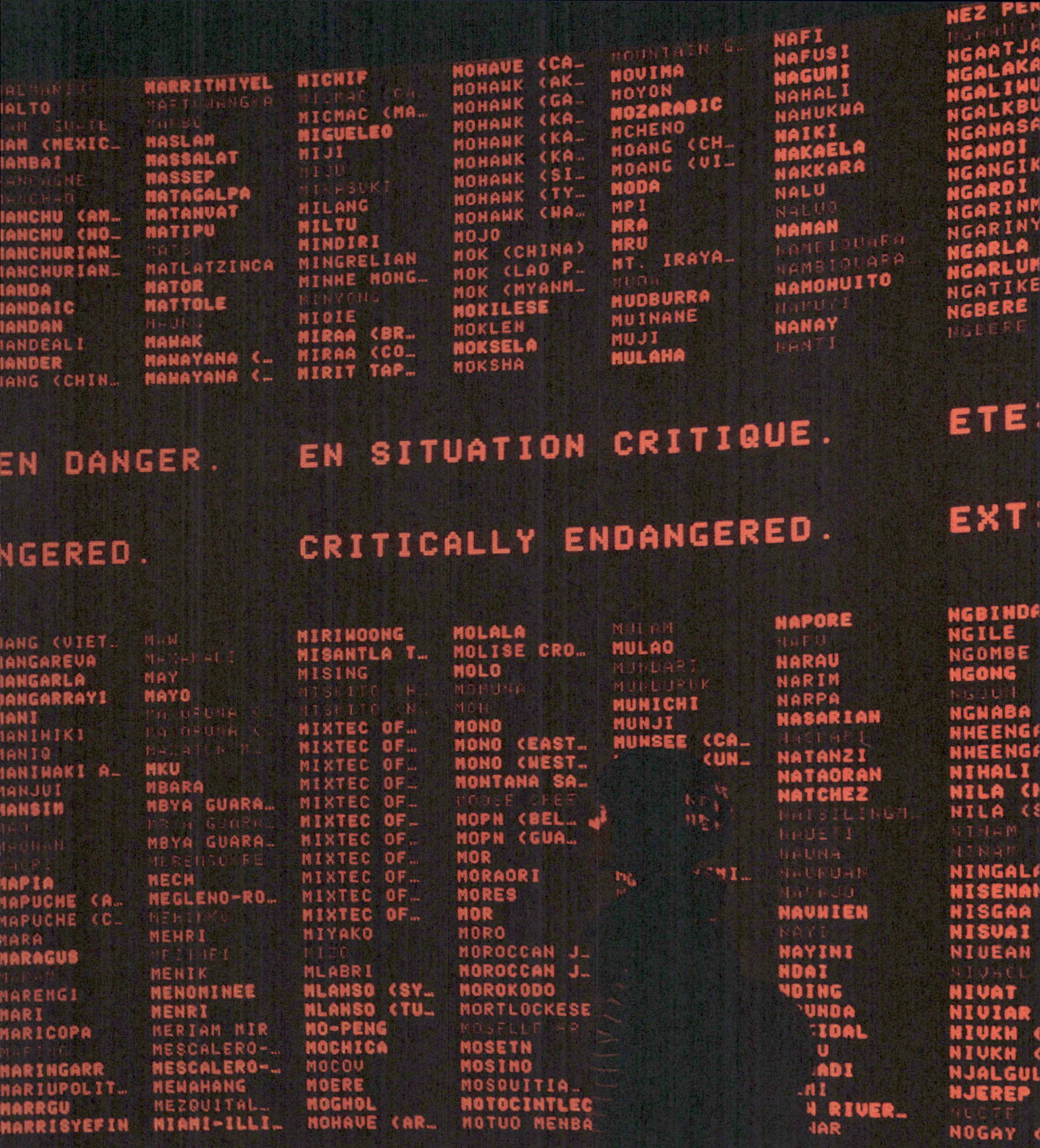

NEZ PER
NAFI
NAFUSI
NAGUMI
NAHALI
NAHUKWA
NAIKI
NAKAELA
NAKKARA
NALU
NAMAN
NAMONUITO
NANAY
NGAATJA
NGALAKA
NGALIWU
NGALKBU
NGANASA
NGANDI
NGANGIK
NGARDI
NGARINM
NGARINY
NGARLA
NGARLUM
NGATIKE
NGBERE
ALTO
AM (MEXIC…
AMBAI
ANCHU (AM…
ANCHU (NO…
ANCHURIAN…
ANCHURIAN…
ANDA
ANDAIC
ANDAN
ANDEALI
ANDER
ANG (CHIN…
MARRITHIYEL
MASLAM
MASSALAT
MASSEP
MATAGALPA
MATANVAT
MATIPU
MATLATZINCA
MATOR
MATTOLE
MAWAK
MAWAYANA (…
MAWAYANA (…
MICHIF
MICMAC (MA…
MIGUELEO
MIJI
MILANG
MILTU
MINDIRI
MINGRELIAN
MINHE MONG…
MIQIE
MIRAA (BR…
MIRAA (CO…
MIRIT TAP…
MOHAVE (CA…
MOHAWK (AK…
MOHAWK (GA…
MOHAWK (KA…
MOHAWK (KA…
MOHAWK (KA…
MOHAWK (SI…
MOHAWK (TY…
MOHAWK (WA…
MOJO
MOK (CHINA)
MOK (LAO P…
MOK (MYANM…
MOKILESE
MOKLEN
MOKSELA
MOKSHA
MOVIMA
MOYON
MOZARABIC
MCHENO
MOANG (CH…
MOANG (VI…
MODA
MPI
MRA
MRU
MT. IRAYA…
MUDBURRA
MUINANE
MUJI
MULAHA
EN DANGER.
EN SITUATION CRITIQUE.
ETE
NGERED.
CRITICALLY ENDANGERED.
EXT
ANG (VIET…
ANGAREVA
ANGARLA
ANGARRAYI
ANI
ANIHIKI
ANIQ
ANIWAKI A…
ANJUI
ANSIM
APIA
APUCHE (A…
APUCHE (C…
ARA
ARAGUS
ARENGI
ARI
ARICOPA
ARINGARR
ARIUPOLIT…
ARRGU
ARRISYEFIN
MAY
MAYO
MKU
MBARA
MBYA GUARA…
MBYA GUARA…
MECH
MEGLENO-RO…
MEHRI
MENIK
MENOMINEE
MENRI
MERIAM MIR
MESCALERO-…
MESCALERO-…
MEWAHANG
MEZQUITAL…
MIAMI-ILLI…
MIRIWOONG
MISANTLA T…
MISING
MIXTEC OF…
MIXTEC OF…
MIXTEC OF…
MIXTEC OF…
MIXTEC OF…
MIXTEC OF…
MIXTEC OF…
MIXTEC OF…
MIXTEC OF…
MIXTEC OF…
MIXTEC OF…
MIYAKO
MLABRI
MLAHSO (SY…
MLAHSO (TU…
MO-PENG
MOCHICA
MOCOV
MOERE
MOGHOL
MOHAVE (AR…
MOLALA
MOLISE CRO…
MOLO
MONO
MONO (EAST…
MONO (WEST…
MONTANA SA…
MOPN (BEL…
MOPN (GUA…
MOR
MORAORI
MORES
MOR
MORO
MOROCCAN J…
MOROCCAN J…
MOROKODO
MORTLOCKESE
MOSETN
MOSINO
MOSQUITIA…
MOTOCINTLEC
MOTUO MENBA
MULAO
MUNICHI
MUNJI
MUNSEE (CA…
NAPORE
NARAU
NARIM
NARPA
NASARIAN
NATANZI
NATAORAN
NATCHEZ
NAVWIEN
NAYINI
NDAI
NGBINDA
NGILE
NGOMBE
NGONG
NGWABA
NHEENGA
NHEENGA
NIHALI
NILA (
NILA (S
NINGALA
NISENAN
NISGAA
NISVAI
NIUEAN
NIVAT
NIVIAR
NIVKH
NIVKH
NJALGUL
NJEREP
NOGAY

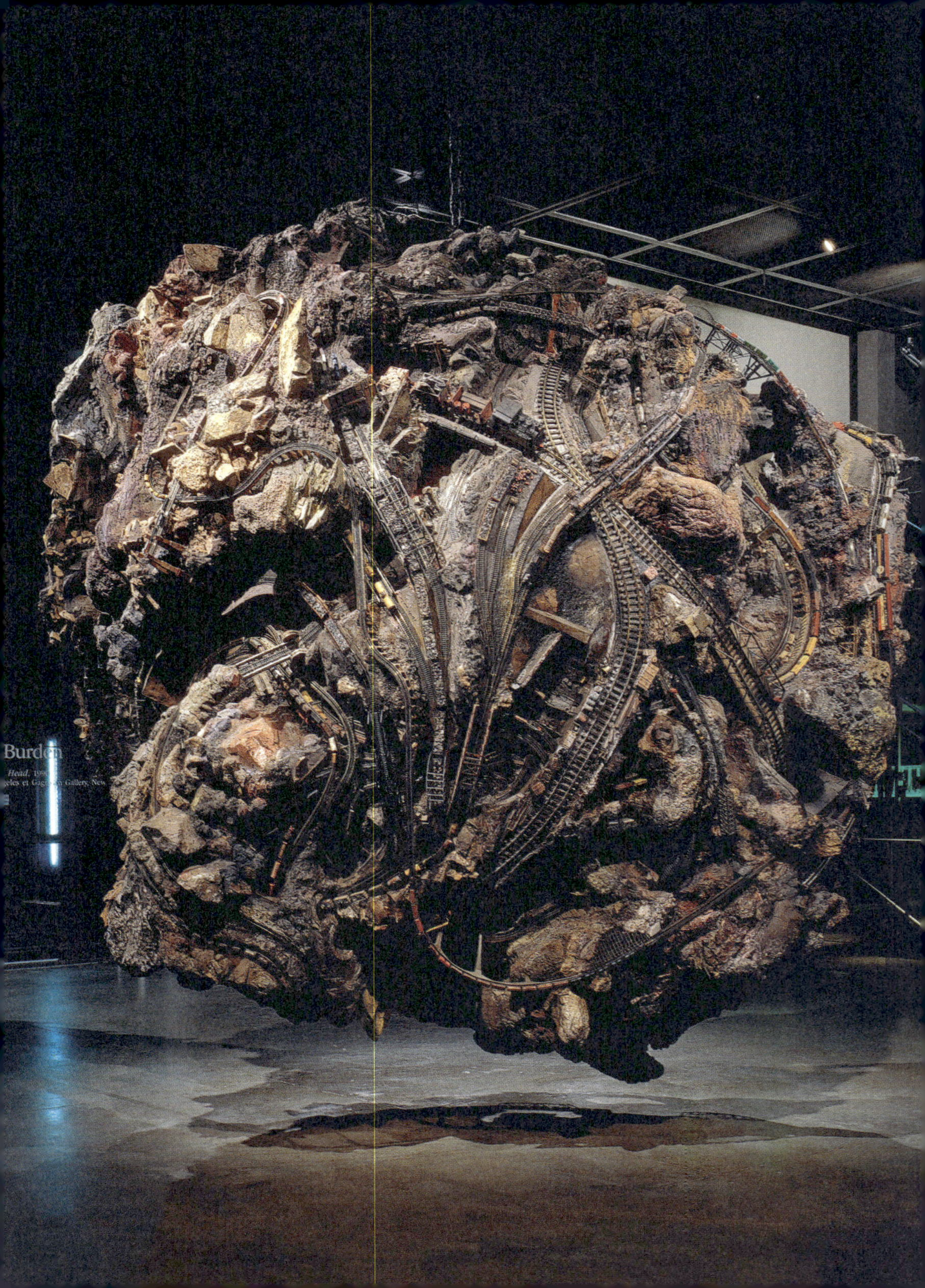
Burden
Head.
Gallery, New

Biographies

Paul Virilio

Paul Virilio (1932–2018) grew up in Nantes, on the western coast of France. During the Second World War, his daily life was marked by routine bombings, an experience that would influence his work. Initially trained as a stained-glass artist, he turned to architecture and cofounded, with Claude Parent, Morice Lipsi, and Michel Carrade the Architecture Principe group in 1963. Professor Emeritus at the École Spéciale d'Architecture (ESA) in Paris, Director and President of this same institution from 1968 to 1998, his teaching was focused on urbanism and architecture. Jean Nouvel, Philippe Lankry, Hala Wardé, and Matthieu Poitevin were among his many students.

An urbanist and essayist specializing in the strategic issues related to new technologies, he became editor of the "Espace Critique" collection at Éditions Galilée in 1973, following the publication of his first philosophical essays. He was awarded the Grand Prix National de la Critique in 1987 by the Ministry of Equipment, Housing, and Territorial Development. In 1990, he became Program Director at the Collège International de Philosophie under the presidency of Jacques Derrida. In the 1980s, Paul Virilio committed himself to the homeless and joined the French government committee for low-income housing (chaired by Louis Besson) in 1992.

Paul Virilio published many books, including *Speed and Politics: An Essay on Dromology* (New York: Semiotext(e), 1977), *Lost Dimension* (New York: Semiotext(e), 1991), *Bunker Archaeology* (New York: Princeton University Press, 1994), *Polar Inertia* (London: Sage, 1999), *The Original Accident* (Cambridge: Polity, 2007), and *Le Littoral, la dernière frontière, entretien avec Jean-Louis Violeau* (Paris: Sens & Tonka, 2013). His writings appeared in numerous French and international publications, such as *Libération*, *Les Cahiers du Cinéma*, *El País* (Spain), *Die Tageszeitung* (Germany), *New Statesman* (United Kingdom), *Artforum* (United States), and *Gaya Scienza* (Japan).

← Chris Burden, *Medusa's Head*, 1990.
Exhibition *Un monde réel*, Fondation Cartier pour l'art contemporain, Paris, 1999

Paul Virilio contributed numerous times as a writer to exhibition catalogs of the Fondation Cartier pour l'art contemporain, namely *Vraiment Faux* (1988), *La Vitesse* (1991), *Azur* (1993), *Un monde réel* (1999), *The Desert* (2000), and *Kelvin 40* (2004). In 2002, he conceived the exhibition *Unknown Quantity*, dedicated to the theme of accident. In 2008, his encounter with Raymond Depardon gave birth to the exhibition *Native Land, Stop Eject*, for which he had the idea of of the installation *EXIT*. Paul Virilio's writings for the Fondation Cartier were gathered in the book *La Pensée exposée*, published by the Fondation Cartier and Actes Sud in 2012.

Unknown Quantity, 2002

In 2002, Paul Virilio conceived specially for the Fondation Cartier an exhibition on the theme of accident. Titled *Unknown Quantity*, this exhibition explored the accident in all its form, from the most ordinary to the most tragic, from natural disasters to industrial and scientific catastrophes. For Paul Virilio, the accident is part of modern history and derives from the phenomena of speed. It is an acceleration that affects life, art, and international politics, and societies that develop speed develop the accident. Thus, *Unknown Quantity* raised the question of inattention on the one hand, namely through Lebbeus Woods's work, *The Fall* (2002), and that of the unexpected on the other, through works by Svetlana Alexievitch, Dominic Angerame, Jem Cohen, Bruce Conner, Cai Guo-Qiang, Peter Hutton, Jonas Mekas, Aernout Mik, Tony Oursler, Artavazd Peleshyan, Nancy Rubins, Wolfgang Staehle, Moira Tierney, and Andrei Ujica.

Native Land, Stop Eject, 2008

Conceived by Paul Virilio and French photographer and filmmaker Raymond Depardon, the exhibition *Native Land, Stop Eject* invited reflection on the notions of being rooted and uprooted, as well as related questions of identity. The exhibition was devised as a confrontation, a contradictory and complementary dialogue between Raymond Depardon, who is very attached to the notions of roots, speech, attentiveness, and land, and Paul Virilio, concerned with the ideas of speed, exodus, and the disappearance of geographic space. In this exhibition, Raymond Depardon questioned the notion of native land in the true sense of the word and its signification today. In order to understand his native land, he confronted it with that of other people in a solo round-the-world trip of fourteen days, from Washington to Cape Town, through Los Angeles, Honolulu, Tokyo, Ho Chi Minh City, and Singapore. He constituted a movie from this trip, which was presented in the exhibition. Also questioning the notion of identity, Raymond Depardon realized the film *Hear Them Speak* (2008) for the exhibition, in which he gave voice to traditional people who expressed their attachment to their native land in their endangered mother languages. In contrast, Paul Virilio examined and challenged the very idea of sedentariness in the face of increasingly complex contemporary human trajectories. The installation *EXIT*, conceived by Diller Scofidio + Renfro, was born from his questioning.

→
Raymond Depardon and Claudine Nougaret, *Hear Them Speak*, 2008. Exhibition *Native Land, Stop Eject*, Fondation Cartier pour l'art contemporain, Paris, 2008

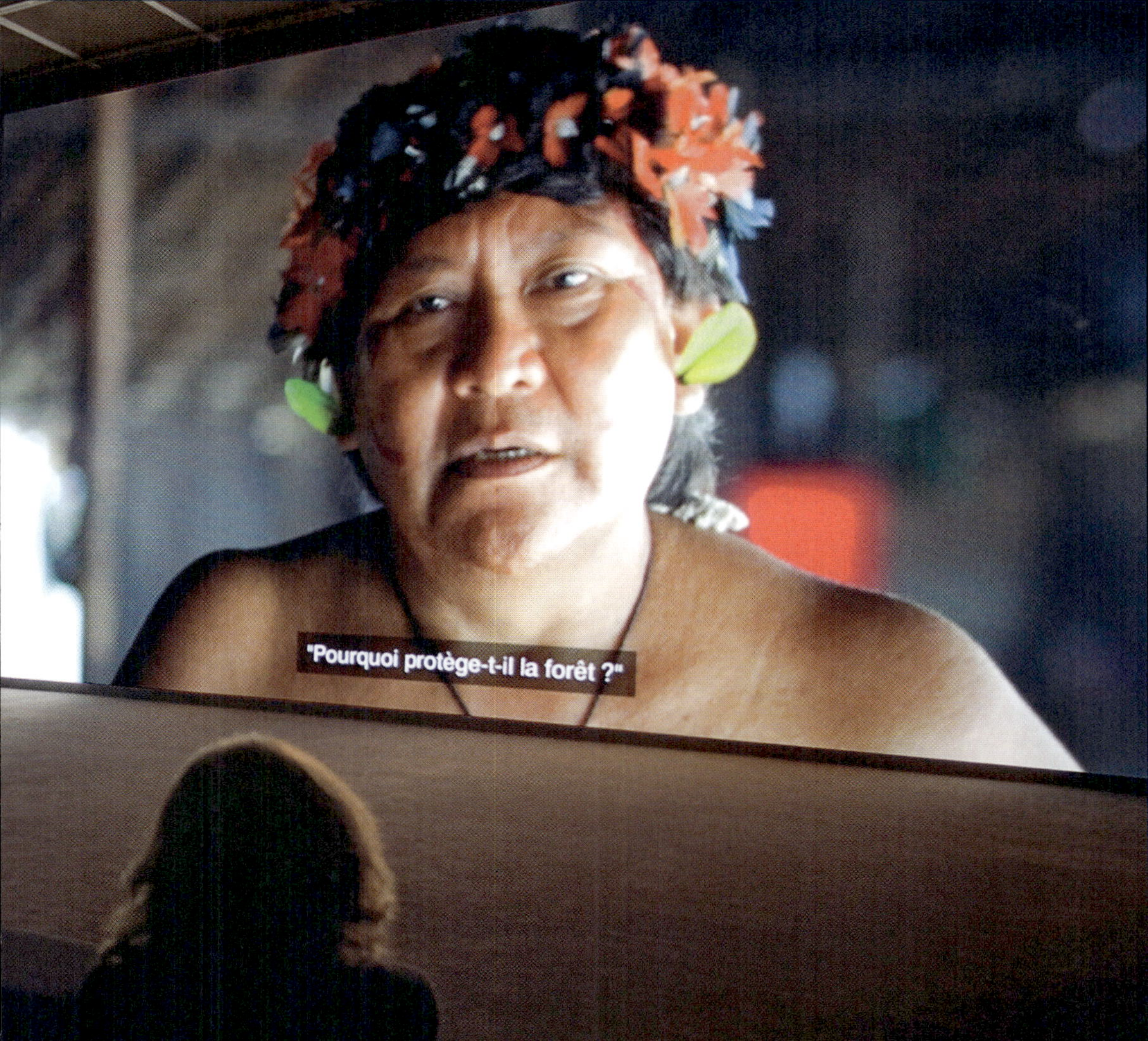
"Pourquoi protège-t-il la forêt ?"

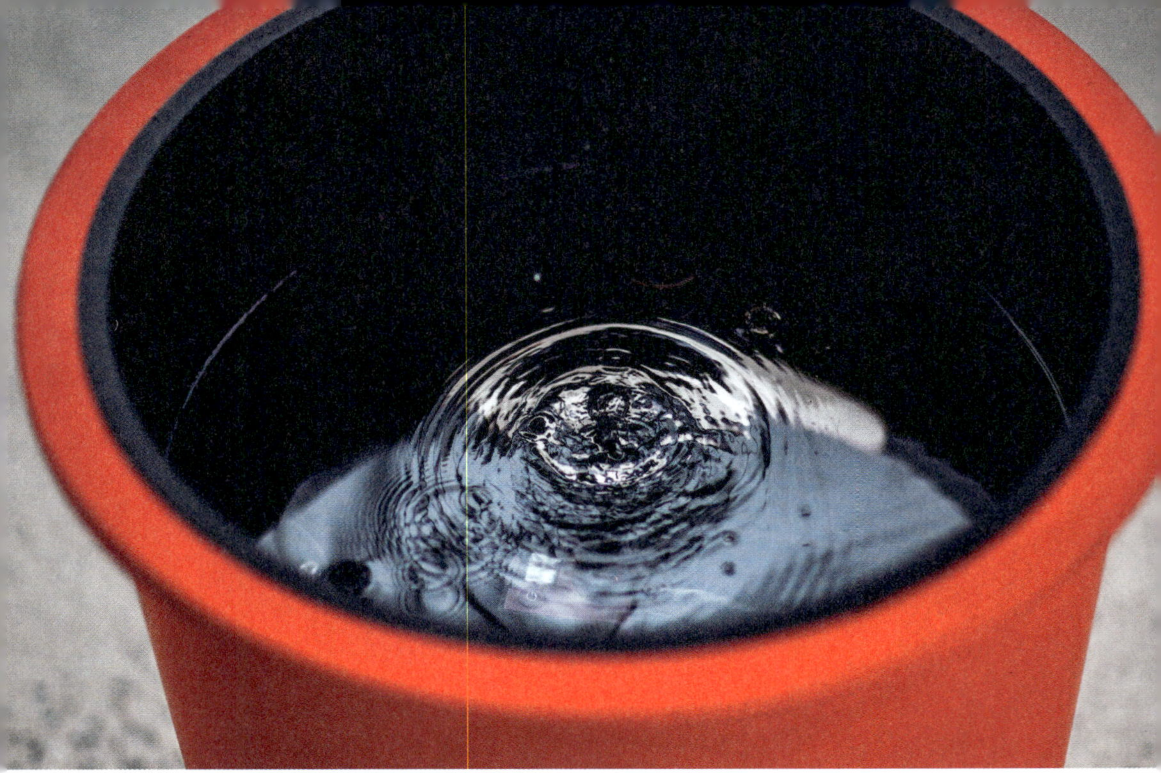

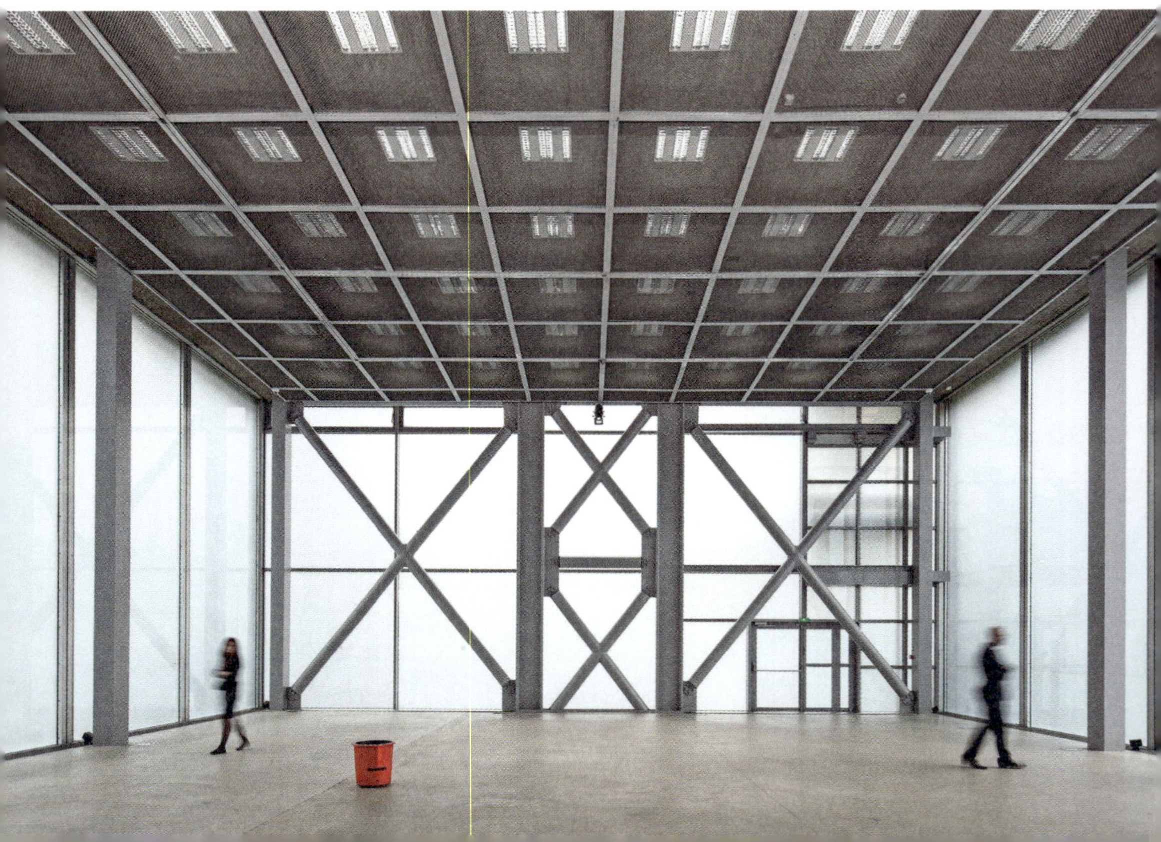

Diller Scofidio + Renfro

Diller Scofidio + Renfro (DS+R) is a design studio whose practice spans the fields of architecture, urban design, installation art, multimedia performance, digital media, and print. Based in New York since 1981, the studio is comprised of over one hundred architects, designers, artists, and researchers, and led by four partners—Elizabeth Diller, Ricardo Scofidio, Charles Renfro, and Benjamin Gilmartin.

DS+R's recent architecture projects in New York include the transformation of the Lincoln Center for the Performing Arts' half-century-old campus in 2010; the High Line in 2014, the adaptive reuse of an obsolete, industrial rail infrastructure into a 2.3-kilometer-long public park; The Shed in 2019, the first multi-arts center designed to commission, produce, and present all types of performing arts, visual arts, and popular culture; and the renovation and expansion of the Museum of Modern Art (MoMA) in 2019. Other significant projects include The Broad museum in 2015, a contemporary art museum in Los Angeles; Zaryadye Park adjacent to the Kremlin in Moscow in 2017; and the London Centre for Music planned for 2020, to be a permanent home for the London Symphony Orchestra.

The studio's recent installation, performance, and curatorial projects in New York include *Charles James: Beyond Fashion* at the Metropolitan Museum of Art in 2014; *Pierre Chareau: Modern Architecture and Design* at the Jewish Museum in 2016; *The Mile-Long Opera: A Biography of 7 O'Clock*, a free choral performance featuring 1,000 singers atop the High Line, co-created with David Lang in 2018; and the Costume Institute exhibition's *Heavenly Bodies: Fashion and the Catholic Imagination* at the Metropolitan Museum of Art in 2018.

For its commitment to merging art, architecture, and culture, DS+R was the first architecture practice to be recognized with the MacArthur Foundation's "genius" grant in 1999. In 2019, the studio was awarded the Royal Academy Architecture Prize by the Royal Academy of Arts in London.

DS+R collaborated with the Fondation Cartier pour l'art contemporain on the exhibitions *Machines d'architecture* in 1992, *Un monde réel* in 1999, *Native Land, Stop Eject* in 2008, and *Musings on a Glass Box* in 2014.

← Exhibition Diller Scofidio + Renfro, *Musings on a Glass Box*,
in collaboration with David Lang and Jody Elff,
Fondation Cartier pour l'art contemporain, Paris, 2014

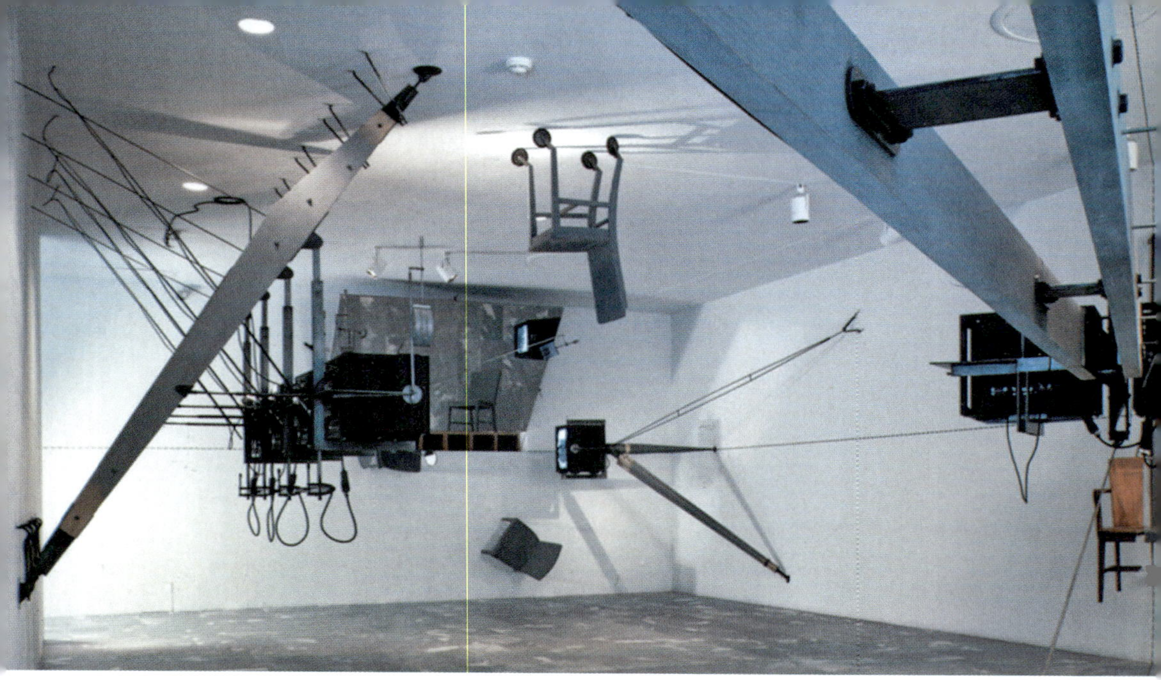

Diller + Scofidio, *Para-site*, 1989. Exhibition *Machines d'architecture*, Fondation Cartier pour l'art contemporain, Jouy-en-Josas, 1992

***Machines d'architecture*, 1992**

The exhibition *Machines d'architecture* was conceived in 1992 with Patrick Javault around a think tank of thirteen international architects, and questioned construction in its relation to life, art, and privacy. It presented the works of architects Donald L. Bates and Kenneth Rabin, Raoul Bunschoten, Elizabeth Diller and Ricardo Scofidio, Bruce Dunning and Pieter Versteegh, Meton Gadelha, John Hejduk, Daniel Libeskind, Ben Nicholson, Jesse Reiser and Nanako Umemoto, who set aside most of their time for drawing, writing, and creating machines that are not preliminary studies waiting to be built but actual works. In that exhibition, Elizabeth Diller and Ricardo Scofidio presented the installation *Para-Site* (1989), consisting of seven surveillance cameras attached like parasites above the entranceways and hallways of the Fondation Cartier, recording visitors' movements. These images were broadcasted on monitors that were installed in a room where convex mirrors and chairs were also suspended in the air. Dashed lines divided the room horizontally and provided a point of reference for the visitor. By electronically connecting remote sites of circulation in the Fondation Cartier, the installation linked self-conscious and unsuspecting viewers in a reflection about looking—the primary activity in the museum gallery.

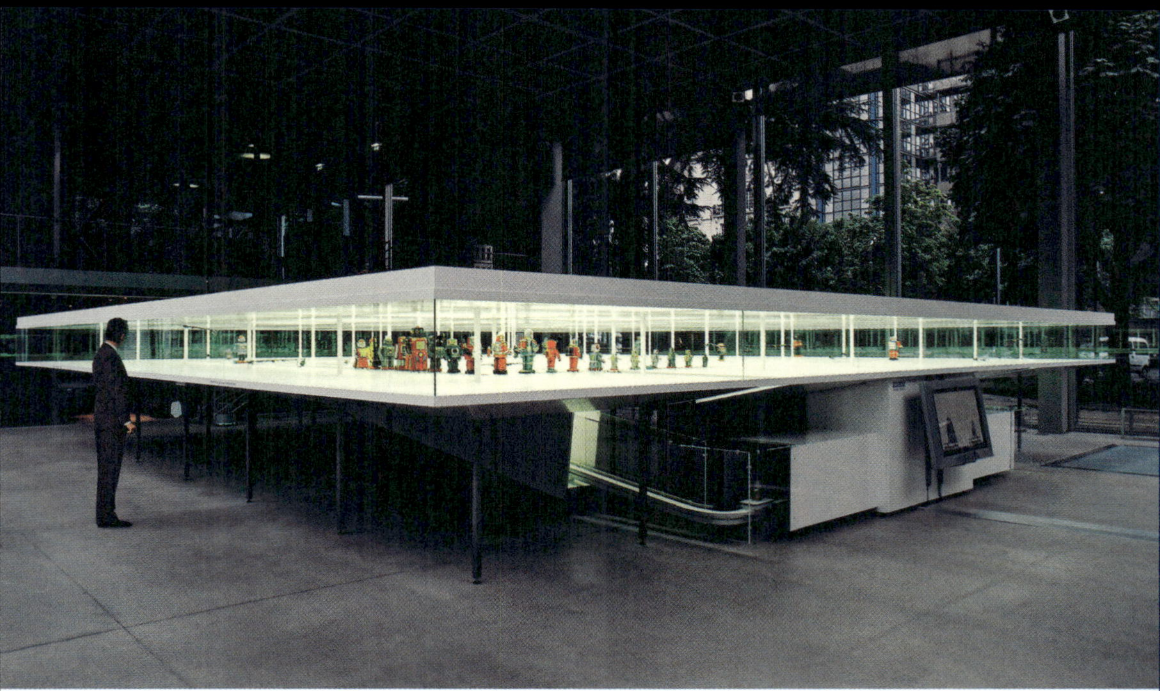

Diller + Scofidio, *Master/Slave*, 1999. Exhibition *Un monde réel*, Fondation Cartier pour l'art contemporain, Paris, 1999

Un monde réel, 1999

Presented at the Fondation Cartier on the eve of the Third Millennium, the exhibition *Un monde réel* explored the relationship between imagination and action, known and unknown territories, the present and dreams, and palpable reality and fiction. Dream machines and spectacular constructions, unknown objects and objects used in space, fictional and documentary films by artists like Jean-Michel Alberola, Beaurin Domercq, Valérie Belin, Chris Burden, James Lee Byars, Cai Guo-Qiang, Bodys Isek Kingelez, Stanley Kubrick, Mœbius, Panamarenko, or Andrei Ujica were at the heart of this exhibition. For that exhibition, Elizabeth Diller and Ricardo Scofidio created the installation *Master/Slave*. Displaying an assembly line of robots from the collection of Rolf Fehlbaum, the installation delves into the pop culture myth of the robot as a surrogate human body that could perform menial tasks and the fear that a machine could acquire enough artificial intelligence to invert the master-slave relationship. Housed in a 90-square-meter glass case, the colony of robots advances on a conveyor belt, often sacrificing direct views with scientific ones—through an airport scanning device that broadcasts robotic entrails and magnified information delivered through a micro-surveillance system.

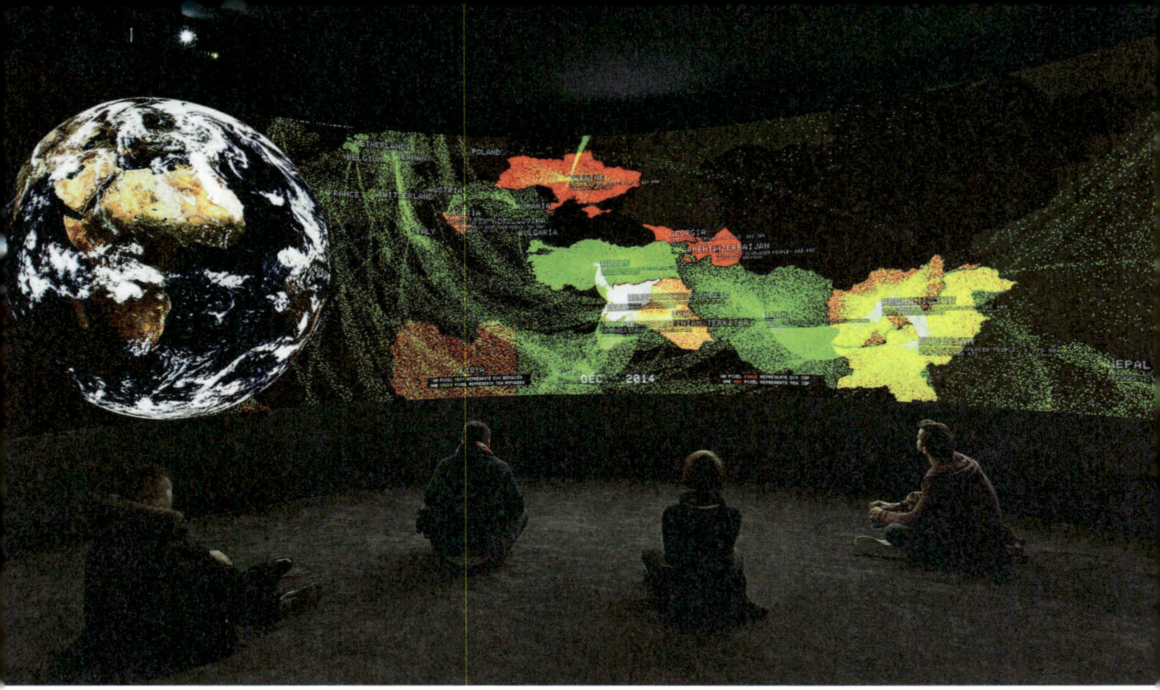

Diller Scofidio + Renfro, Mark Hansen, Laura Kurgan, and Ben Rubin, in collaboration with Robert Gerard Pietrusko and Stewart Smith, *EXIT*, 2008. Exhibition *Native Land, Stop Eject*, Fondation Cartier pour l'art contemporain, Paris, 2008

Native Land, Stop Eject, 2008

Born from a conversation between Paul Virilio and French photographer and filmmaker Raymond Depardon, the exhibition *Native Land, Stop Eject* proposed a reflection on the notions of being rooted and uprooted, as well as related questions of identity. It established a complementary dialogue between Raymond Depardon, who questioned the notion of identity and native land, namely through his film *Hear Them Speak* realized for the exhibition and in which he gives a voice to those who wish to live on their land but are threatened with exile, and Paul Virilio, who reflected on the very idea of sedentariness in the face of the unprecedented migrations confronting the contemporary world. It was on this occasion that Diller Scofidio + Renfro, Mark Hansen, and Laura Kurgan conceived the installation *EXIT*, which immerses the viewer in a dynamic presentation of the data documenting contemporary human movements.

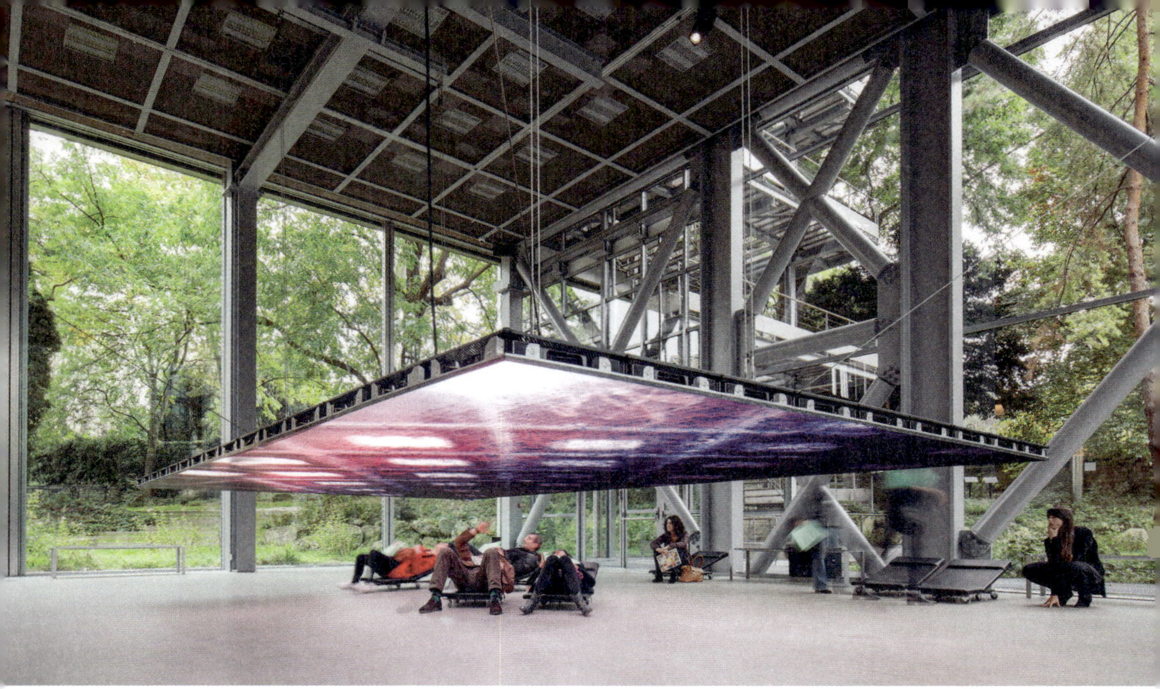

Exhibition Diller Scofidio + Renfro, *Musings on a Glass Box*,
in collaboration with David Lang and Jody Elff,
Fondation Cartier pour l'art contemporain, Paris, 2014

Musings on a Glass Box, 2014

On the occasion of the thirtieth anniversary of the Fondation Cartier in 2014, Diller Scofidio + Renfro imagined *Musings on a Glass Box*. Jean Nouvel's distinctive glass exhibition spaces in the Fondation Cartier have been a provocation to artists and curators for more than two decades, upending the conventions of the white box gallery and pushing the limits of architecture. The large, transparent walls of the building were at the forefront of glass technology in the 1990s, aspiring to one of Modernism's highest goals: to dematerialize the wall and seamlessly connect interior to exterior. Using a cliché of time lapsed and the appearance of neglect, *Musings on a Glass Box* began with a single leak from the ceiling of the Fondation Cartier. A response ensued with the aid of a bucket, a chorus, sensors, robotics, remote communications, video, and real-time sound processing. The two ground floor galleries were interconnected in a feedback loop. Small gestures in the Fondation Cartier's large gallery were amplified in its smaller one, making the familiar seem uncanny and turning the banal into the grotesque. The project was a collaboration with composer David Lang and sound artist Jody Elff.

Mark Hansen

Holding a Bachelor's Degree in Applied Mathematics from UC Davis and a PhD and a Master of Art in Statistics from UC Berkeley, Mark Hansen joined Columbia Journalism School in New York in July 2012, where he directs the Brown Institute for Media Innovation and teaches mainly advanced data analysis. He began his career as a member of the technical staff at Bell Laboratories in Murray Hill and as a professor in the Department of Statistics at UCLA.

For nearly three decades, Mark Hansen has been working at the intersection of data, art, and technology. He has been awarded eight patents and has published over sixty papers in data science, statistics, and computer science.

His work with Ben Rubin and Jer Thorp has been exhibited at the Whitney Museum of American Art in New York, the Museo Nacional Centro de Arte Reina Sofía in Madrid, the Science Museum in London, the Fondation Cartier pour l'art contemporain in Paris, the Museum of Modern Art in New York, and is permanently displayed in the lobbies of the New York Times and the Public Theater in New York.

Laura Kurgan

Laura Kurgan is an Associate Professor of Architecture at the Graduate School of Architecture Planning and Preservation of Columbia University, where she heads the Center for Spatial Research and the Visual Studies curriculum. In 2004, she founded the Spatial Information Design Lab at GSAPP, which she directed until 2015. She is the author of *Close Up at a Distance: Mapping, Technology, and Politics* (New York: Zone Books, 2013) and co-editor of *Ways of Knowing Cities* (New York: Columbia Books on Architecture and the City, forthcoming).

Her work explores the ethics and politics of digital mapping and its technologies; the art, science, and visualization of big and small data; and the design of environments for public engagement with maps and data. It has been shown at the MACBA in Barcelona, the ZKM in Karlsruhe, the Fondation Cartier pour l'art contemporain in Paris, the Museum of Modern Art in New York, the Palais de Tokyo in Paris, the Venice Biennale, the EXPO Chicago, and the XXII Triennale di Milano. In 2009, Laura Kurgan was awarded a United States Artists Rockefeller Fellowship.

Robert Gerard Pietrusko

Holding a Bachelor of Music in Music Synthesis from the Berklee College of Music in Boston, a Master of Science in Electrical Engineering from Villanova University, and a Master of Architecture from the Graduate School of Design at Harvard University in Cambridge, Robert Gerard Pietrusko is an engineer-designer focusing on the relationship between contemporary technology and spatial products. He is an Associate Professor in the Department of Landscape Architecture at the Harvard Graduate School of Design, where his teaching and research focus on geographic representation, simulation, narrative cartography, and the history of spatial data sets.

Robert Gerard Pietrusko's design work has been exhibited worldwide, at venues such as the Museum of Modern Art in New York, the ZKM in Karlsruhe, and the Venice Biennale.

Ben Rubin

Ben Rubin is a media artist and an Associate Professor of Design at the New School for Social Research in New York, where he directs the Center for Data Arts. He holds degrees from Brown University in Providence and the MIT Media Lab in Cambridge.

Ben Rubin uses data, computation, and media to engage with pressing social and cultural issues, creating public installations and environments for performance, radio, film, and exhibitions. His work has been presented at venues including in New York the Lincoln Center for the Performing Arts, the Museum of Modern Art, and the Whitney Museum of American Art, the ZKM in Karlsruhe, and the Museo Nacional Centro de Arte Reina Sofía in Madrid. He has received commissions from institutions including the New York Times and the Public Theater in New York, and the University of Texas in Austin, as well as various prizes including an Obie Award, a Webby Award, a Golden Nica Award, and an Excellence in Design Award from the New York City Public Design Commission.

Stewart Smith

Holding a Master of Fine Arts in design from Yale University, artist Stewart Smith has worked with Google's Creative Lab and Data Arts teams, Unity Technologies, and Amazon's Sumerian group. He is the founder of the technology and strategy consultancy Moar Technologies Corp. His artwork has been exhibited at the Fondation Cartier pour l'art contemporain in Paris, the Museum of Modern Art in New York, the ZKM in Karlsruhe, the SFMoMA in San Francisco, and has appeared in publications such as *Domus* (Italy), *Esquire* (United States), and *Creative Review* (United Kingdom).

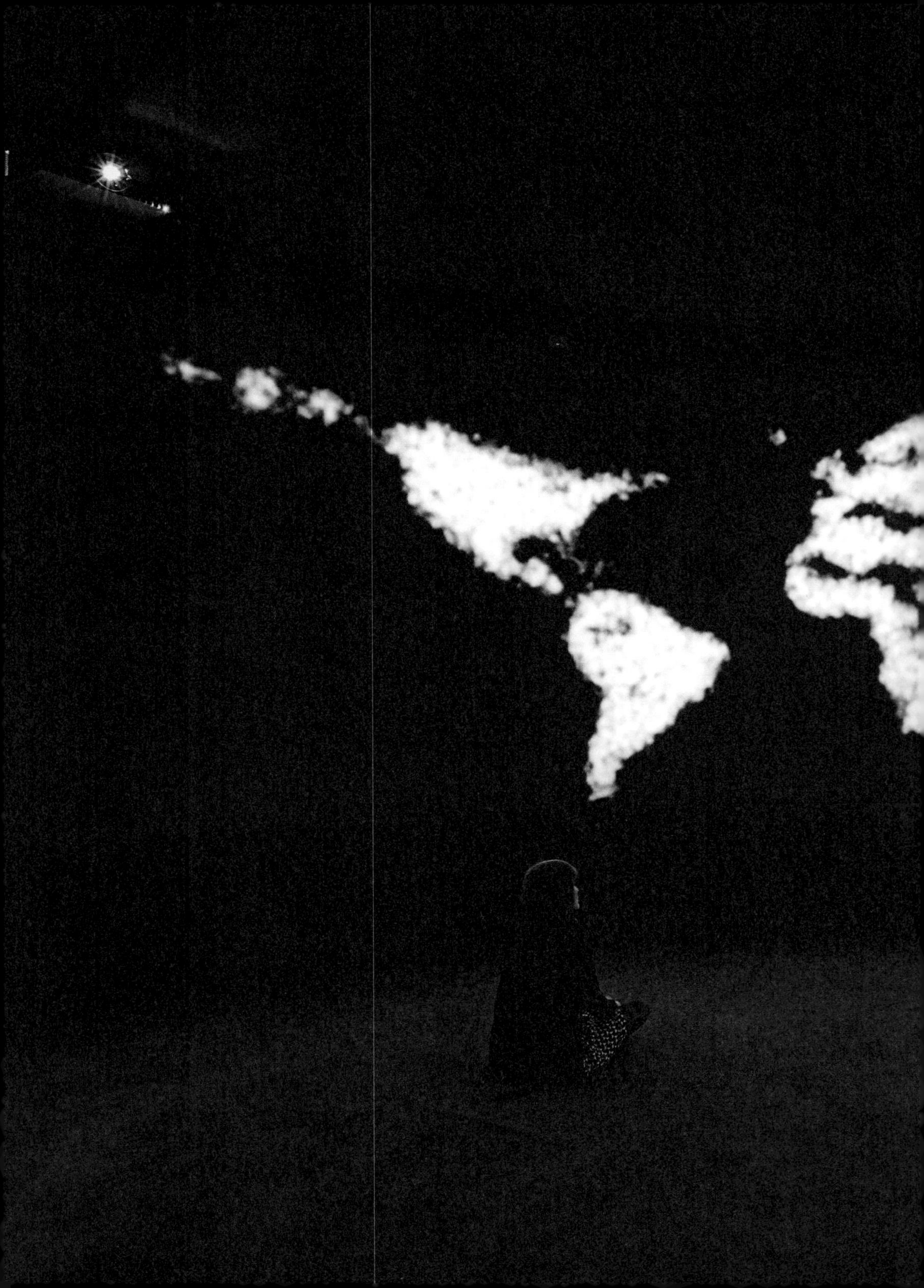

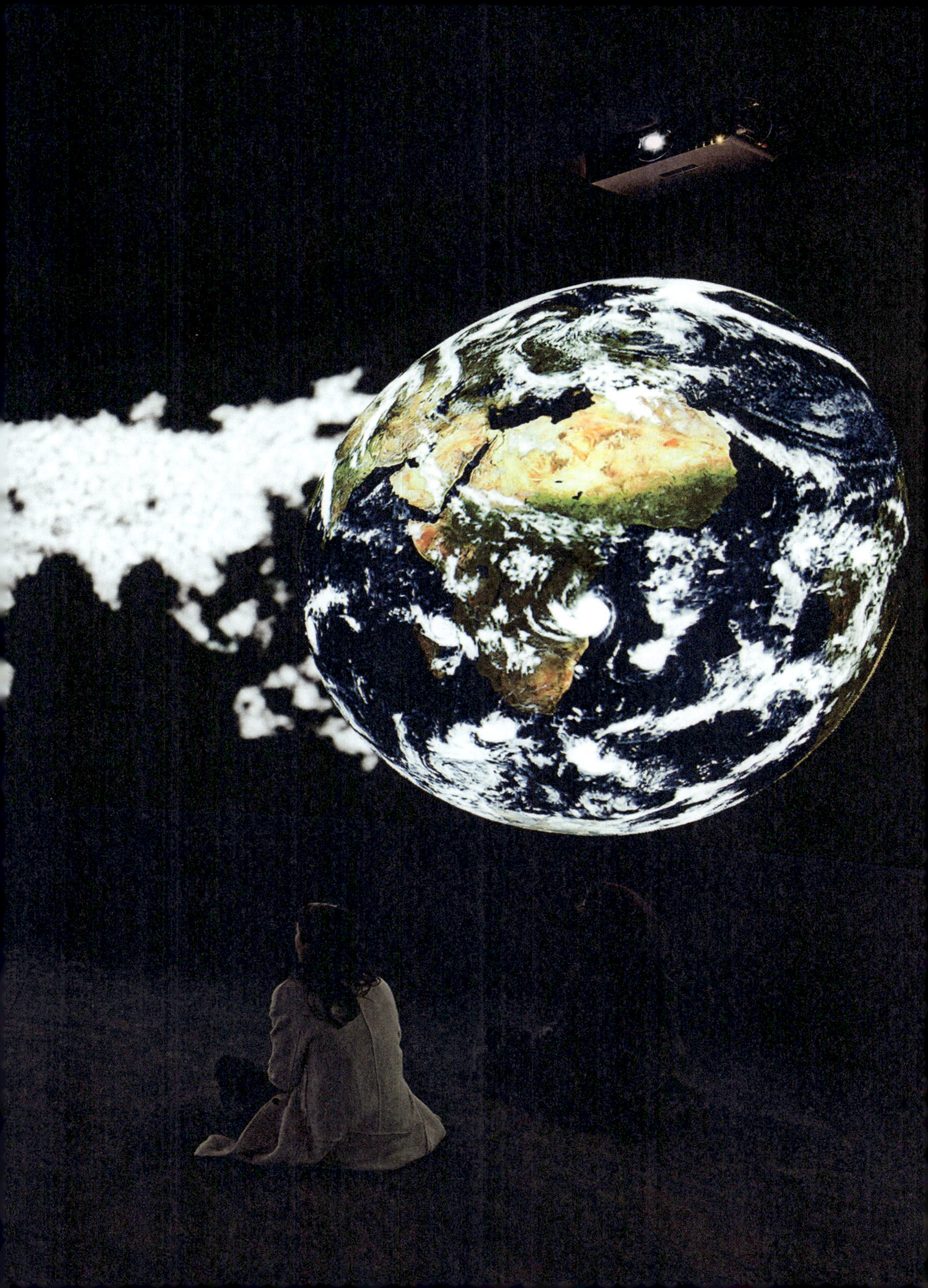

For their contribution to the elaboration of the cartography of the work *EXIT*, thanks to:

Askarinta Adi, IT and GIS Coordinator, Komunitas Konservasi Indonesia Warsi
Regina Below, **Bernadette Dubus**, and **Dr. Debarati Guha-Sapir**, École de Santé Publique, Université Catholique de Louvain
Nicolas Chavent, UN Joint Logistic Centre, Rome
Robert Chen, Director, Center for International Earth Science Information Network (CIESIN), Columbia University, New York
Marcus Colchester, Director, and **Jake Willis**, Advisor, Forest Peoples Programme, Moreton-in-Marsh, United Kingdom
Amanda Cox and **Steve Duenes**, Graphics Department, *The New York Times*, New York
Jeff Crisp, **Yvon Orand**, **Henrik Pilgaard**, and **Luc St-Pierre**, United Nations High Commissioner for Refugees (UNHCR), Geneva
Eric Howard, Center for Embedded Networked Sensing, University of California, Los Angeles
Zachary Forest Johnson, Program in Cartography and GIS, University of Wisconsin, Madison
Tann vom Hove, City Mayors, Freiburg, Germany
Diane Lambert, Statistics Research, Google, Los Angeles
François-Michel Le Tourneau, Centre de recherche et de documentation sur l'Amérique latine, UMR 7169, CNRS, Paris
Kytt MacManus, GIS Specialist, Center for International Earth Science Information Network (CIESIN), Columbia University, New York
Malte Meinshausen, Potsdam Institute for Climate Impact Research
Hanson Njiforti, Country Director, and **Gaston Buh Wung**, GIS Coordinator, World Wildlife Fund, Cameroon

Acknowledgements

Dr. Manuel Orozco, Inter-American Dialogue, Remittances and Development Program, Washington DC
Federica Ranghieri and **Fatima Shah**, The World Bank, Washington DC
Yann Rébois, CartONG, Chambéry, France
Carlos Alberto Ricardo, Director, **Diego Pinheiro de Menezes**, GIS analyst, and **Rodrigo Gravina Prates Junqueira**, Agronomist, Instituto Socioambiental, São Paulo
Colin Rundel, UCLA Statistics, University of California, Los Angeles
Juan Francisco Saldarriaga and **Madeeha Merchant**, Associate Research Scholars, and **Jonathan Izen**, Research Assistant, Center for Spatial Research, Columbia University, New York
Oyvind Sandbukt, anthropologist, Archipelago Ecoservices Ltd.
Yumiko Uryu, Advisor, World Wildlife Fund, Indonesia
Tom Wigley, Climate and Global Dynamics Division, University Corporation for Atmospheric Research, Boulder, United States
Sarah Williams, Spatial Information Design Lab, GSAPP, Columbia University, New York

Thanks also to:
Alhóndiga Bilbao, Bilbao
Forest Peoples Programme, Moreton-in-Marsh, United Kingdom
Instituto Socioambiental, São Paulo
Komunitas Konservasi Indonesia Warsi
United Nations Educational, Scientific and Cultural Organization
World Wildlife Fund

EXIT, 2008–2015

Duration: **45 minutes**
Installation diameter: **8.8 meters**
Installation height: **4 meters**

Foreword by Paul Virilio, La Rochelle, 2008
Digital video
Duration: **3.21 minutes**

An idea by **Paul Virilio**
Research and design: **Diller Scofidio + Renfro**, **Mark Hansen**, **Laura Kurgan**, and **Ben Rubin**, in collaboration with **Robert Gerard Pietrusko** and **Stewart Smith**

Collection of the Fondation Cartier pour l'art contemporain, Paris

Created at the initiative of the Fondation Cartier pour l'art contemporain for the exhibition *Native Land, Stop Eject*, 2008
Chief Curator of the exhibition: **Hervé Chandès**
Curator of the exhibition: **Ilana Shamoon**

Scientific Consultant: **François Gemenne**

Scientific Consultants on the map *Speechless and Deforestation*:
Bruce Albert, Director Emeritus of Research, Institut de recherche pour le développement (IRD), Marseille, France
François-Michel Le Tourneau, Senior Research Fellow, Centre national de la recherche scientifique (CNRS), Paris
The map *Speechless and Deforestation* was produced by the **Alhóndiga Bilbao**, Bilbao, in collaboration with **UNESCO**.

Production of the foreword by Paul Virilio: **Axelle Poisson**

No dataset is neutral: the information in *EXIT* has been collected by various organizations for specific policy and research purposes. While mindful of the work each organization has undertaken to produce the data, the authors of *EXIT* have intentionally refunctioned them to build a narrative about global migration and its causes.

Presentations of *EXIT*

April 25—July 29, 2018
***Fondation Cartier pour l'art contemporain. A Beautiful Elsewhere*,**
Power Station of Art, Shanghai

October 26—November 10, 2017
XX Bienal de Arquitectura y Urbanismo de Chile, Valparaíso

May 31—August 15, 2017
***Highlights: La Collection de la Fondation Cartier pour l'art contemporain*,**
Seoul Museum of Art, Seoul

April 22—July 13, 2017
Shanghai Himalayas Museum, Shanghai

April 19—July 16, 2017
Ian Potter Museum of Art, University of Melbourne, Melbourne

January 7—March 25, 2017
UNSW Galleries, University of New South Wales, Sydney

November 25, 2015—January 10, 2016
Palais de Tokyo, Paris

May, 18—August 1, 2010
Alhóndiga Bilbao, Bilbao

December 19, 2009—February 21, 2010
Kunsthal Charlottenborg, Copenhagen

November 21, 2008—March 15, 2009
***Native Land, Stop Eject*, Fondation Cartier pour l'art contemporain, Paris**

Publication

Graphic Design: **Nolwen Lauzanne, Paris**
Editorial Coordinator: **Cécile Provost**
Editorial Assistant: **Aubane Favier**
Copy Editor: **Bronwyn Mahoney**
Production: **Géraldine Lay, Actes Sud, Arles**
Photoengraving: **Daniel Regard, Les Artisans du Regard, Paris**

Fondation Cartier pour l'art contemporain, Paris

Credits

EXIT

© Diller Scofidio + Renfro, Mark Hansen, Laura Kurgan, and Ben Rubin, in collaboration with Robert Gerard Pietrusko and Stewart Smith

Foreword

p. 40: photo © Silversalt

Population Shifts: Cities

pp. 4, 43 (1), 44–47: photos © Diller Scofidio + Renfro, Mark Hansen, Laura Kurgan, and Ben Rubin, in collaboration with Robert Gerard Pietrusko and Stewart Smith

pp. 6–7, 100–101: photos © Luc Boegly

Remittances: Sending Money Home

pp. 39, 43 (2), 48–51: photos © Diller Scofidio + Renfro, Mark Hansen, Laura Kurgan, and Ben Rubin, in collaboration with Robert Gerard Pietrusko and Stewart Smith

p. 36: photo © Grégoire Eloy, Tendance Floue

Political Refugees and Forced Migration

pp. 43 (3), 52–55, 72: photos © Diller Scofidio + Renfro, Mark Hansen, Laura Kurgan, and Ben Rubin, in collaboration with Robert Gerard Pietrusko and Stewart Smith

p. 96: photos © Luc Boegly

Natural Disasters

Cover, pp. 43 (4), 56–59: photos © Diller Scofidio + Renfro, Mark Hansen, Laura Kurgan, and Ben Rubin, in collaboration with Robert Gerard Pietrusko and Stewart Smith

pp. 22–23, 78: photos © Luc Boegly

Rising Seas and Sinking Cities

pp. 43 (5), 60–63: photos © Diller Scofidio + Renfro, Mark Hansen, Laura Kurgan, and Ben Rubin, in collaboration with Robert Gerard Pietrusko and Stewart Smith

pp. 32–35, 82–83: photos © Luc Boegly

Speechless and Deforestation

pp. 43 (6), 64–67: photos © Diller Scofidio + Renfro, Mark Hansen, Laura Kurgan, and Ben Rubin, in collaboration with Robert Gerard Pietrusko and Stewart Smith

pp. 68–71, 86–87: photos © Luc Boegly

Other Works

p. 8: © Lebbeus Woods and Alexis Rochas, photo © Daniel Janin / AFP
p. 24: photo © Olivier Ouadah
p. 88: © 2019 Chris Burden / licensed by The Chris Burden Estate and Adagp, photo all rights reserved
p. 91: © Palmeraie et désert, photo © Grégoire Eloy, Tendance Floue
p. 92: © Diller Scofidio + Renfro, in collaboration with David Lang and Jody Elff, photo © Will Chafkin (1), photo Luc Boegly (2)
p. 94: © Diller + Scofidio
p. 95: © Diller + Scofidio / Collection Rolf Fehlbaum, Basel, photo © Valérie Belin / Adagp, Paris, 2019
p. 97: © Diller Scofidio + Renfro, in collaboration with David Lang and Jody Elff, photo © Luc Boegly

Printed and bound by CPZ SpA, Cenate Sotto, Italy, in June 2019.

Fondation Cartier pour l'art contemporain
261, boulevard Raspail, 75014 Paris, France
fondation.cartier.com

Distributed in the United States of America
by Thames & Hudson Inc.,
500 Fifth Avenue, New York, New York 10110

www.thamesandhudsonusa.com

ISBN 978-2-86925-143-4

Distributed in all other countries, excluding France,
by Thames & Hudson Ltd,
181A High Holborn, London WC1V 7QX

www.thamesandhudson.com

ISBN 978-2-86925-143-4

Printed and bound in Italy